QUEST
—*for the*—
GRAIL

✠

QUEST
— *for the* —
GRAIL

RICHARD ROHR

A Crossroad Book
The Crossroad Publishing Company
New York

1997

The Crossroad Publishing Company
370 Lexington Avenue, New York, NY 10017

Copyright © 1994 by Richard Rohr

Printed in the United States of America

Library of Congress Cataloging-in-Publication Data

Rohr, Richard.
    Quest for the grail / Richard Rohr.
    p. cm.
    ISBN 0-8245-1411-4; 0-8245-1654-0 (pbk.)
    1. Spiritual life—Catholic Church. 2. Grail. 3. Men—Religious
life. 4. Masculinity (Psychology) I. Title.
BX2350.2.R643 1994
248.8′42—dc20   94-3372
                                                    CIP

Contents

Editor's Note

Anyone who has ever sat in front of a compelling speaker knows the truly eloquent can ruin a good sentence just by completing it. Body language comes into play. Pregnant pauses whisper meanings that on the printed page must be written between the lines. The shrugging of a shoulder or raising of an eyebrow send the meaning ahead of the words, and this allows the speaker who is a genius to bend the language while mesmerizing the audience.

Father Richard Rohr's *Quest for the Grail* began life as a retreat. So the words in this book were, in the first place, spoken. Moreover, they were not spoken in a cozy chapel but in the context of a men's rugged week amid mountain and forest. The words, therefore, sweat and grunt at times. There's a touch of John the Baptist about them. In translating the magic and grace of that week to the more sedate and proper printed page, an occasional grunt had to be muted, an occasional sentence rounded out. But, wherever possible, the original "voice" was allowed to remain. The reader would do well to "hear" the words as if spoken on a hillside while the sun goes down, a latter-day sermon on a mountain near you.

The retreat was for men, and so the language is not always as inclusive as it otherwise might be. This original focus has been maintained — with the hope that both men and women will find the insights to be helpful.

Someone called the poet Shelley a "light leaper from crag to crag of inexpressible fancy." Richard Rohr is a light leaper from insight to insight — above syntax, beyond logic, probing at truths we only half suspected, hinting at possibilities most of us, in our very average lives, do not dare dream, the fresh images leaping over old rules and restrictions and going for the gusto.

Not so much a book as a trip on the mountain.

—MICHAEL J. FARRELL

Preface

Here begins the descent. Here begin the terrors and the miracles. Here begins the quest.

— Perleslaus

I am told that the quest legends emerged in Europe in a variety of forms from around 1180 until 1350 C.E. They originated from various levels of society. They developed at precisely the time when the great Gospel story was in eclipse and no longer reaching the ears or affecting the souls of baptized Christians. So the Grail stories were lay persons' ways of charting and describing the necessary and good spiritual path.

Since the story was neither canonized nor condemned in any particular form, it continued to grow unfettered and uncensored. The myth expressed the deep wisdom of the Christian collective unconscious, although now in a style that was neither churchy nor clerical. Neither did it waste time being anti-church or anti-clerical. Instead, these stories moved boldly into a world of mystery and metaphor. They could do this with confidence because the quest was real, the myths anchored in reality. It was Catholic lay spirituality at its best.

I believe we are living at a time when the quest is *not* real. Our people are unsure of the goal, insecure in their search for meaningful patterns, and even unconvinced of any divine origins. It is a major crisis of meaning for the West, and at the deepest level it is a loss of hope.

Most people do not frame the problem in this way, but I am convinced that both the anxiety and the solutions to it are subterranean and cannot be addressed at a mere surface or

9

problem-solving level. Only sacred psychology or mythology are deep and true enough to address the questions of meaning and hope.

Since there was never an official form of the quest story, I was able to draw upon a number of tellings. It was largely an oral tradition that encouraged the soul to express itself without doctrinal presuppositions, orthodox restrictions, or clerical interference. Today, I am trying to do the same and, not so surprisingly, encountering a sort of super-orthodoxy, at least with regard to the classic and enduring themes of faith and morals.

The three great streams of the story flowed through German, French, and English traditions. I have drawn upon all three and cannot promise the scholars that I will be consistent in following any of them. There is a bit of Wulfram von Eschenbach's *Parsifal,* some of Chrétien de Troyes's version, and a taste of the Arthurian legend.

There is also some twentieth-century awareness of archetypal psychology, the genius of Carl Jung, Joseph Campbell's monomyth of the hero, Catholic liturgical symbolism, and my own intuitions. The past is benefit and limitation, as is our own private experience. The best we can do is recognize our sources and own our biases as we chart a course for the soul.

We will have been true to the quest tradition if these pages stir the reader to do the same. Perhaps we are burdened with rewriting the quest for the Holy Grail in every age and generation.

Insofar as this myth is a lay creation, handed down primarily by the laity, destined to be addressed, in our own time, primarily to the laity, it is salutary to remember that the term "lay" is not diminutive or pejorative, but perhaps an indication of advantage and head start in spiritual matters. "Beginner's mind" is always open to learning and conversion. Too much "teaching church" leaves one smug and superior. Jesus was a layman. And he described the quest pretty well! Religious professionalism often confuses the quest with role, custom, or group identity, which really are not much of a quest — they raise no "questions"!

I am writing this brief introduction sitting next to the death bed of my mother, and on my first manual typewriter from the 1950s.

Waves of memory, grief, and nostalgic joy wash over me as I look out at this Kansas prairie and recall the safe and comforting myths I grew up with: Mom and Dad were together and forever, life worked if you worked hard enough, most people were good and honest, evil and failure were the exceptions, life was as reliable as this old typewriter, and you could probably avoid the tragic by being rational and responsible.

There was really no need — or expectation — for "descents," "terrors," or even "miracles."

For the most part, these half-true myths worked and got me through to the half-century. Now the eternal earth woman who bore me gasps for breath, and this first typewriter makes an awful lot of mistakes, with no correcto-type to undo them.

The essentially tragic nature of human life took a long time to reach this protected land of Oz. But it did. Myths keep us safe from the truth, but they also keep us safe *for* the truth — until the soul is ready and the time is right for the full message. I guess I am ready. "Everything belongs" has become my motto and mantra.

I am ready to believe and even trust things at fifty that I would have tried to fix at thirty or forty. The stories finally do their job, but the chapters make most sense if read in order.

The Grail story can be told and retold, but finally it is a quest and must be walked. It is always a descent, always a terror, and for those who know the bigger story, always participation in a miracle.

The work of religion is to awaken the soul so that it will be ready when the teacher arrives or when the Messiah comes. Healthy religion does this through the magic of word and image. Catholics called it sacrament. It taught us how to see, how to see everything, and how to see everything all the way through. It told us that the quest was real, that myths were not myths at all in the contemporary sense, and that there really is hope and meaning hiding behind the tragic.

Theologian Father David Tracy says that Catholics, or at least what I call "great Catholics," have a symbolic advantage over many of their Jewish and Protestant friends. He says the true Catholic, formed by the great tradition of symbol, image, literature, saint, and history, tends to *imagine differently*, to interpret all events within a different universe of meaning than others in the Judeo-Christian tradition.

Tracy says we tend to see all events and things as analogous to the divine. He calls it the "analogical imagination." The "great Catholic" does not see God as apart, above, beyond, different from, against, in judgment on; but amazingly sees God as with, in communion with, choosing for, like, similar in pattern, and compassionate toward all that is human and created.

For some wonderful reason, Catholicism tends to take the incarnation with absolute seriousness. One sees it in our best art, architecture, fiestas, poetry, literature, social life, liturgy, and ever recurring readiness to proclaim forgiveness, exception, compassion.

One sees the incarnation especially in a unique Catholic sense of time, process, and journey. There is always grace between the bridge and the water. Mistakes are often mystery — working themselves out in time.

Nowhere is this taught more completely and more "audibly" than in this homespun story of a man growing up, learning the right questions, through trial and temptation, as he pushes on toward God. Every person or event he encounters is a necessary and grace-filled occasion. There are no dead ends, there is no wasted time, no useless characters or meaningless happenings. *All* has meaning; it is still an enchanted universe; God is in all things waiting to speak and even to bless.

In the quest, God speaks and leads through family, failure,

violence, visitors, betrayal, sexuality, nature, shadow, vision. It is clearly and brilliantly a layman's journey unto God. For once, the language makes sense to *men*, who have for too long found Catholic "sanctuary talk" to be without muscle, merit, or meaning.

Thanks to the patient editing of Michael Farrell, we bring this wondrous myth to modern men in post-modern times (when the myth has fallen apart). Our hope is that you will find hope here. I have seen many men find it as I tell the story widely to crowds of male questers.

We have to keep telling the story of our Catholic forefathers. No civilization has survived unless the fathers see it as their task to give hope and meaning to the next generation. Here we write for the sons, and we wait for the sons to ask the right questions and make the quest real.

Our Journey with Parsifal

Separation & Departure — The all-embracing Mother
Search for the Father

Early preparation — The Five Knights (Encounter with maleness)
Devastated Monastery (Encounter with Spiritual emptiness)
Nameless Woman (Female conquest)
Red Knight (Male conquest)
Horse and Armor (Living out of image)
Gournamond (Positive Father who gives him the right question)
White Flower (Positive Feminine encounter)

The Grail Castle (First Initiation) — The Fisherman Guide
Amfortas/The Fisher King (Wounded Maleness)
The Grail King (Whole Maleness/ The Father/God)
The Procession
Man with sword
Man with bleeding lance
Woman with Grail (still veiled)
Baptismal initiation
No question asked

The Deepening Spiral (Encounter with Shadow self) — The laughing woman
The weeping woman
The accusing woman

The Dark Knight/Vassal
The Wise Old Man

Wandering/Avoidance/ Denial — Parsifal's forty years in the desert
Good Friday/Blood Price/ Axis Mundi

Return to the Castle (Unveiling of the Grail/ Living with Grail King) — The Hermit Guide (Journey internalized)
Heals Amfortas
Asks the Question
Holy Marriage is complete (with self, the opposites, and God)

When the inner King rules:	*When the inner Queen rules:*
Inner patriarchy	Inner matriarchy
Objectivity is preferred	Subjectivity is preferred
Reason and law	Meaning and exception
Pattern	Repair
Spirit-truth	Soul-remembrance
The public good	The personal good
Outer order/healing	Inner healing/order
House	Home
Loyalty to the Big Story	Loyalty to my inner story
Language of responsibility	Language of rights
Determined	Compassionate
Becomes too big/outer/ objective	Becomes too small/inner/ subjective
Moves toward structure	Moves toward chaos
Outer authority	Inner authority
Breadth/Height	Depth/Synthesis
Holds together the Whole	Authenticates the parts
Fate/duty/obligation	Beauty/pleasure/feeling
Ties us to the past	Connects us to the now
Form	Content
Beyond me	Within me
Cold truth/hard	Warm truth/soft
The container	The contents
The substance	The symbolism
Order before caring	Caring before order
Driven by the goal	Driven by the journey
Tradition	Experience
Thought over feeling	Feeling over thought

We are living in an imbalanced time: The structures are still patriarchal, but the mood and language is that of the Queen. The form is all King and the content is an overcompensating Queen — a very privatized language of pathology, criticism, victimhood, and romantic sympathy — driving the King function into "a blessed rage for order." As always, each side has half of the truth. We wait and work for "holy marriage" in individuals and in institutions and societies.

Glossary for Chapter 2

Prophet: That part of a man that deconstructs and drops out of the conventional wisdom. He directs and legitimates "the path of the fall."

Priest: That part of a man which believes and affirms ultimate meaning, transcendence, and union. He directs and legitimates "the path of the return."

King: That part of a man that holds all the other parts together in unity and wholeness. He directs and legitimates the bigger picture, the real, the "realm." (One must participate in some "king energy" to be an adequate or good father.)

Warrior: That part of a man that can say no to himself, and to others, for the sake of a more important goal. He directs and legitimates an appropriate sense of boundaries and a needed sense of "enemies." (Essentially dependent on the wisdom of a good king/father.)

Magician: That part of a man which understands the inner world of mystery, metaphor, paradox, and growth. He directs and legitimates the work of the soul, issues of darkness, light, and shadow.

Lover: That part of a man which tastes, enjoys, appreciates, and creates beauty and connectedness. He legitimates ultimate joy by participating in it now.

Hero: Either (1) the early-stage warrior who is "building his tower" or (2) one who stays on the whole path through all its stages until the end, his wounds becoming "sacred" and transformative.

Tragic hero: Either (1) one who fails to see his wound as a "sacred wound" or (2) one who does not know who he is, but merely who he is supposed to be. The modern celebrity who is well-known merely for the sake of being well-known.

Tower: The early heroic instinct that drives a young man to be generous, disciplined, earnest. Sometimes an even fanatical or rigid need for order, morality, black-and-white worlds — so he can rise above hedonism and selfishness. Good and necessary up to a point, until a wise king is allowed to broaden him, a magician to deepen him, a lover to soften him.

Faith: The gift that encourages one to build the tower, and then later to descend the very tower that he has built. Looks different in each stage. First is "ego-morality" and second is "soul-morality," preparing one for the takeover of Spirit.

Glossary for Chapter 4

Ego-consciousness: That part of me which pushes forward from what it *thinks* to be true. It is effective, driven, and necessary, especially in the first half of life, to "build one's tower." Becomes blind and egocentric when we think that's all there is.

The unconscious: That part of me (and reality) that I am unaware of but is still operative. Untapped without self-knowledge, suffering, and inner work that calls ego-consciousness into question. Source of most of our motivation, moods and creative breakthroughs. The well and deep stream of our humanity.

The anima ("soul"): The feminine part of a man, which is largely carried and often hidden in the unconscious, unless called forth by the outer feminine (mother, women friends, wife, balanced men, images, biographies). It is the source of men's sensitivity, capacity for rich relationship, nuanced feeling, poetry, and religion.

The animus ("spirit"): The masculine part of a woman, also largely carried and often hidden in the unconscious, unless called forth by the outer masculine (father, male friends, husband, balanced women, images, and biographies). It is the source of women's confidence in the outer world of things, objectivity, detached judgment, and the transcendence of spirit.

Anima attack ("The wimp in whirlpool"): When a man is pulled into the negative side of the feminine, where he is ill at ease and insecure. He becomes moody, petty, sarcastic, sentimental or withdrawn, because he is out of his element. To come out, he must know what he is really feeling and find a way to express it in an outer relationship.

Animus attack ("The witch ascending on her broom"): When a woman is pulled into the negative side of the masculine, where she is ill at ease and insecure. She becomes opinionated, makes harsh judgments and sweeping generalizations, is unfocused, and manipulates logic. Moves into angry scorn when men do not understand. To help free her, we must let her say what is *really* bothering her, which she is herself out of touch with, as shown by her overstated opinions.

The sword:
    Negatively: Power, domination, violence, and control. Competition for its own sake. The warrior disconnected from a good king, wise magician, or tender lover.
    Positively: The male ability to clarify, decide, and separate issues, emotions, and personalities. The good side of judgments, analysis, and detachment. The "art of separation" that preserves healthy autonomy and avoids codependency.

Chapter 1

Who on earth are we? _____

The American Plains warriors, according to ancient legend, used to say in the morning: "It's a good day to do great things." To be able to say that and mean it was a magnificent ambition. Such an aspiration stirs something deep in the heart of any young man who would strive to be a hero.

Is there a hero in the house?

A hero, for the record, is not a saint, much less a god. In the great mythologies and legends, the hero is always an ordinary human being, with at least one tragic flaw. A hero is one who simultaneously keeps his eye on himself and on a goal beyond himself — a goal often, but not always, called God.

Furthermore, one can be a hero in only one place. One can be a hero only of one's own story. One can't be the hero of St. Francis's story. This heroism, in other words, is not achieved by dreaming.

The journey to happiness involves finding the courage to go down into ourselves and take responsibility for what's there. All of it. This means looking at the self without flinching, owning up to whatever wreckage we find, but also acknowledging that there are some promises there, that there is some energy there, some life there.

The aim is to experience the fact that *everything belongs* — the good, the bad, and the ugly. Often this is hard — especially coming to terms with the ugly — and may take living a while. At almost fifty, I am beginning to realize that more clearly. I can see myself better. At twenty-five, I had no strong sense that everything belonged, but it did and it does.

Without getting too dramatic, I believe all this is vitally important for the churches. The Catholic Church and Western civilization generally are in a state of spiritual emergency. I have never known a time when so many people were leaving the church. I have never known a time when so many people were living under such massive illusion. And I find myself overwhelmed by that. Our civilization is no longer producing heroes.

Heroes may be wretched, awful, sinful, tragic, but they are never small. Occasionally one meets someone cast in that heroic mold in the most unlikely places, perhaps at an Alcoholics Anonymous meeting: wretched perhaps, but not small. There is clearly a worthwhile soul there.

The aim here is to do soul work. It must be distinguished from the work of spirit, although these two obviously need one another.

Such soul work, if taken seriously, is no picnic. The pain of the hero is heart-rending. And, to make coping harder, it is mysterious, often even to the hero himself.

I don't think we're failing to produce heroes because we are suddenly a selfish people and unlike other ages and cultures. It is not because we are narcissistic or materialistic, though we are both and may find it easy to blame these things.

A world of dead symbols

The problem is, we are a people with no symbolic universe.

The hero always exists within a mythic universe in which his heroism is defined and summoned forth. What has happened in recent times is that the cosmic egg is broken. The cosmic egg was a fancy phrase for a coherent world in which things fit and make sense. In the coherent world there was a creation story, and everyone had a path; even if it was some-times wrong, there was a path down which we all struggled together.

We no longer have the luxury of such a mythic world. We occasionally get excited about an individual or an event, a president or a war. We are desperately hankering for what Rollo May calls "a mythic universe" within which to stand and make our lives heroic and crown them with relevance.

Myth is something that never was but always is. The late scholar and author Joseph Campbell did us a great service through his research into mythology. He was born Catholic, which he said gave him a great head start, but equally sig-nificant was the fact that he later became disillusioned with Catholicism because, he said, the Catholic Church lost the imaginal world.

Once, the world of images was at the heart of Catholicism. But, in recent centuries, a more rational, left-brain mental-ity took over Western civilization, including most of our religious institutions. A more technical way of thinking pre-vailed. Myth does not speak that sleek, cool language of the pragmatic. It speaks the soaring, undisciplined language of pictures and story.

All the language of religion is to be found in myth. This poetic imagery is the language of the soul. It opens up spaces within us.

This is the language and world we must try to redis-cover in these pages. It must be a team effort, a communal search. I can play metaphorical drums, but the reader must do the listening and opening up and eventually decide what drumbeat to follow.

This endeavor will not succeed if we stay in the same old, self-conscious shell where we have grown comfortable, and persist in playing roles and thinking along lines that are conventionally correct and considered acceptable. The world where the myth is reborn, and where the creation story again makes sense, normally happens when today's conventions are thrown out the window. And here's the challenging part: It happens where tragedy and the strains of silence are found.

Joseph Campbell's writings reminded us we have not understood or appreciated myth since the Enlightenment. Most of us grew up with a notion of myth as something that is not true. Wrong. There is nothing in the world truer than myth.

Furthermore, without myth people disintegrate psychologically. This can be validated in culture after culture, tribe after tribe. Destroy the mythic universe, and the psyche quickly begins to deteriorate. All the indices say ours is a rapidly deteriorating culture. Sickness, addiction, neuroses, desperation, and suicide are everywhere. Because the soul just cannot be held together.

I am convinced that if the Christian myths most of us were raised with were still alive and well, and if we had access to those myths, we would be a highly energized and productive people. When a myth is cooperative, there is endless creativity.

Between 1150 and 1250 C.E. in France, for example, people undertook, in the midst of an impoverished economy, the building of hundreds of cathedrals, which usually took three generations to complete, but which still stand as masterpieces in little towns. Sometimes their cost was the entire economy of the city. Only a century of mythic conviction could cause so much creativity to explode.

Gothic cathedrals express a harmonious world where God is enthroned on the altar. It is also a world of gargoyles and monsters, a world with a dark side. It acknowledged good and evil wrapped in one worldview.

And most of those French edifices were called "Notre Dame." Our Lady. The people were entranced by the woman, the feminine. And not "My Lady" but "Our Lady." They understood their peoplehood. They lived community.

The soul has normally been seen as "feminine": ethos rather than logic, poetry rather than prose, image rather than concept. The way to the holy for any man is through such an image world — not through the world of logos or reason. Instead, the world of eros opens up undreamed spaces, fires the imagination. That's why men write poetry when they fall in love — because the soul comes alive at that moment.

In the past several hundred years, however, we have tried to do an end run around the soul, and around the body, to get to spirit. It doesn't work. Soul and spirit are not the same thing. But do an end run around soul and body, and you won't necessarily get spirit. All you'll get is cheap religion, which is what we have now, where soul-work is not taken seriously, where the body is not appreciated or integrated. (No wonder so many leave the church for groups that legitimate soul and body.)

The Christ myth a caricature

For the church, right or left, the Christ myth is not dominant. Neither the so-called conservatives nor the so-called progressives are in a period of zeal — each side simply projects its own massive shadow on the other. When we are filled with myth and story, we do not worry about what side we are on. A Grail experience is just too alive for inter-group fighting and turf battles, for church politics in all its everyday pettiness.

Because we lost the great mythic universe, we find ourselves in a post-Christian era dominated by rationalism, with its desire to understand and control. So we lack a mythic language that is nature-based or mystery-filled. Mythic language is always pointing outward and upward. It explains how we are situated in a bigger picture or bigger story.

When you don't mythologize, you pathologize. All you have left is to write your own little story. When it goes awry, you get therapy and recover. But, after overcoming sickness, drinking, or whatever, what then? Recovery alone is not the point: We don't have a mythology for a bigger, better world to "recover" to.

We have to concede that the old church prior to the Second Vatican Council did at least provide people with a clear myth. The theology may have been sentimental devotionalism, but you were told where you came from, where you stood, and where you were going. That was all the mind needed. In fact, one Grail experience was enough. Once you knew there was an alternative world, *you knew*.

This takes us back to the old Baltimore Catechism, which taught that we are created to know, love, and serve God in this world and be happy with him (*sic*) in eternity — something like that. That is very good and simple. Whoever believes that (and a great many don't believe such myths anymore) has at least a world, a meaning system, to cling to. Without such an assumption of reality, the burden falls on you to find a substitute. You then have to create your own story. As long as you are not plugged into the Great Life, you are lost in an insignificant life.

Western people today are lost in their insignificance. Thus, to take a ridiculous but also a typical example, people dye their hair purple, trying to be "someone." They're looking for an identity. They have to be outrageous and rebel in order to make a mark. The burden is upon each little ego, each little psyche, to create significance. And when we fail to do that, there is shame or lack of self-esteem. We cannot, apart from the wider universe, make ourselves significant. Modern secular people are necessarily burdened with low self-esteem.

The Greeks had a word for it

The effort to make ourselves significant is what Greek tragedy calls "hubris," a brand of pride. Every hero in every Greek tragedy finally falls because he does not recognize that pride. "Arrogance" might be a better word. That tragic flaw still can destroy us. That's why I teach the enneagram, to let people see we all have this flaw, which is also a gift, and that we can be destroyed by our gift.

One of the great mythic systems that shape Western civilization is Christianity. Even Carl Jung, although not a full believer, advised caution before throwing out the Jewish-Christian tradition. But most people today do not listen to such warnings. Here in New Mexico, people don feathers and change their name to Prairie Dog to create their own mythology.

Such games are plain hubris. The individual is saying, in effect, that he will not carry his own history. It is folly to assume that all his ancestors were heretics and stupid, and he of course is not. Trying to find who we are apart from this sinful, broken but wonderful history is a waste.

Most of us, probably for good reasons, do not want to carry the burdens and darkness of our history. We were confronted in 1992 with the five hundredth anniversary of the arrogance that made us "discoverers" of a new world. Our one and only past did form us — it is who we are. We need to own up to it to acknowledge all that we are.

Groups are usually held together, whether we like it or not, by both totems and taboos. Gangs have much to do with symbols: flags, mottos, slogans, metaphors. You confront my image or my color, man, and you are dead. That is my meaning system. Myths operate on a non-rational and even irrational level. But they are still the things that people die for.

Similarly, on a broader spectrum, what we are dealing with in, for example, the Democratic and Republican national conventions are massive culture wars. They represent two cultures that no longer understand one another. They can have the same words but interpret them out of different mythologies, and indeed both meanings may be hidden from the rest of us. This can happen without anyone going crazy because our mythic universe operates largely at an unconscious level.

I remember one of our professors in the junior seminary

whom we dreaded as a rigid disciplinarian. We asked him one day, "Father, who is your hero?" His answer, without hesitation: General Patton.

Why would this man become a Franciscan? He had the brown robe, all the symbols, but nothing in his life even approximated what St. Francis loved or stood for. I am not saying he was not a good man. But his mythological universe was General Patton, not St. Francis. His real world relied upon domination and control. These were the values and virtues he cherished, although he was probably unaware of it.

I visited him as he lay dying. I think it is fair to say he died a very unhappy man. No one ever helped him put the pieces together, so his soul wasn't allowed to operate with any kind of truth or freedom.

There is a deep level at which it is okay to be "me," and it goes beyond the cheap cliché. It is equally okay to be "us" as a community. As things stand, we don't have much of an "us," so we devise artificial ways, such as making wars, that give us that sense of "us" against some "them." Men's gatherings are trying to remedy that loss of our sense of us. Gender images are the most profound polarities of the soul. These are the final taboos and the first fascination. No other images match the power of maleness and femaleness — and that is the power of the movements afoot today. We will give up other choices and values when those images are at stake. And because those paradigms are in major transition right now — major transition — we men are running scared. It is as if men are now asked to find meaning in an instant.

Man behind the eight ball

What do the male symbols mean? What is good about being a man? What is good in the "other half" of God? Whatever and whoever God is, half of it is masculine. We have to discover that half of the mystery. To see that it is good must be our work, our challenge. We are living in a period with a high degree of what someone called "misandry" — a hatred of men.

I am white and educated and American and male and ordained — in other words, I'm in big trouble. For many people, these are now a burden and a problem. In some quarters, just to be male, without making any other distinctions, is to be set up for criticism. It is sad to find oneself in such circles, where all evils supposedly come from the male.

In this scenario, for some reason, the feminine is inherently virtuous, and the masculine by nature evil — some commentators are getting very close to saying just that. And some of us are getting very close to believing it. Men are feeling very beaten-up and insecure about being men. Imagine the destructive effect this has on young men and boys.

Myths are also the foundations for moral values. The moral arena is presently dominated by the pro-life, pro-choice impasse on abortion. The two groups have invested in two mythologies and now stand screaming at one another for the cameras.

There are Catholics on both sides of the abortion issue. What they do not recognize is that, underneath the surface, each is operating out of a different symbolic universe. Until we can address that, there is no point on the rational level in fighting about pro-life or pro-choice. They cannot understand one another.

What true religion has always done is open the door to this symbolic universe, to the world of the soul that is the primary access point for the spirit world. We can see who we really are by taking responsibility for both God on the altar and the gargoyles on the corners. We must realize both are part of the picture. Then we cannot call people on the other side the gargoyles. We cannot say all the evil is over there. A whole new kind of civil dialogue may then emerge because the ego is out of the way.

Although the sacred journey is a communal quest, it must nevertheless start for me with my little life. I have to be preoccupied with my health, with my importance, with making a living. I also must decide who is good and who is bad, and what is good and bad. Every myth starts that way, with the personal details.

Then the little man, laboring to write his private story, sees defeat entering his life. There always has to be the sacred wound. It may be a disease, a failure, a disaster, loss of a loved one. It is often described in the stories as a broken heart. The world does not make sense anymore. There is, as it were, a film over the world, throwing it out of focus. Life is not hopeful, does not have any juice to it.

Living with the wound

This journey was expressed in abbreviated form in the initiation rite for young men. The rite evolved so that the young man could later recall the wound and make allowance for it. This phenomenon, the ritual humiliation of the young male, is found in every culture, whether it is Native American, Greek, Chinese, African.

Such a ritual, when the would-be hero was called upon to endure pain, usually happened at the age of twelve or thirteen. The Judaic tradition, in which this moment was symbolized by circumcision, is typical. It is amazing that such a strange gesture would emerge in so many diverse cultures.

Some day, when we encounter setback or defeat, if we can recall this wounding and integrate it, the memory may move us from pathology into mythology. Such integration would enable us to see the self as part of a bigger picture.

But if — and this is what often occurs today — the wound does not lead to the bigger story and only to enduring and grieving, then it becomes an embittering scar that sends us back into the private self to curse our bad luck. To illustrate the value of proper perspective, here are two accounts of the *same* young life; one is merely factual, one is mythic and sacred:

1. I was born into an average family. My mother was a schoolteacher and my father was a conductor on a railroad. As the youngest child, no one paid much attention to me. My mom was away working all day, and my dad on the train would be gone for days at a time. One day, I ran away into the woods and stayed there for three days. I enjoyed being with the squirrels and rabbits. But when I got back, my father beat me with a strap until the blood came. My brothers and sisters would not talk to me, and my mother did not seem to care. At that point I began to fail in school, and the teachers told me I was stupid.

2. Once upon a time, there was a very special child, born with a promise and a bright light within. His mother, who knew the ways things worked, was often away helping the poor, and his Dad traveled on caravans to distant realms. So the boy would go to the forest, where he was recognized by the animals and birds. Once he stayed there for several days, experiencing the joy of being accepted in the forest. When he returned home, he was tortured until he forgot his true identity. For years he wandered, lost in mists, bumping into giants until, crushed and broken, one day he could see (and so on).

In the first account, the boy is wounded and embittered; in the second, the same wounding has become ennobling and even sacred.

Most myths include belief either in a benevolent universe, a hostile universe, or one that is indifferent. Until we accept that ours is a radically benevolent universe, we are not Christians. Going to Mass does not make one Christian. I don't think the General Patton–type friar knew it was a benevolent universe. He had to control a hostile world of little fourteen-year-old seminarians who might take away his power.

We cannot stay in the indifferent universe for long. It will soon deteriorate into the hostile universe. Instead, if we are lucky, we will finally meet what we call grace, the notion that *someone is for me more than I am for myself.* That is the first Grail being unveiled. I feel an aura of synchronicity and providence; things seem to work. It is radically okay.

When, for a time, I lived in a hermitage, I felt animals were talking to me. That must sound crazy, but Franciscans talk like that. I would stand on my porch, and these animals would move right up to watch me. It was for me a new beginning of aliveness. I was realigned with reality and the universe was re-enchanted.

It better be a good world

The work of religion is to open our eyes to see such realities in a world where everything swirls with meaning. Thus, we need to take time out, time apart in silence, so the soul can start seeing again, and listening. And then we realize we are part of a much bigger story.

If we keep getting trapped in the little story, and the little wound, it will become the embittering wound. Heroes thank God for the wound. Our contemporary non-heroes, instead, go on "Oprah" to cry or complain, or we sue for millions of dollars, because we got this little wound, we were humiliated, we were cheated — no heroes will come from such a culture, and no greatness.

We should carry the wound like a badge, for years if necessary, even when it does not make sense, and we don't even make sense to ourselves. That's how we move gracefully into the sacred story.

Chapter 2

What you going to do
with that tower, son? _____

The drum has emerged as a resounding symbol and expression of the new male consciousness movement.

Because of the type of person I am, product of our pragmatic American culture, fortified by a good rational education, I thought at first the drumming was sort of hokey and was skeptical about the claims that it so consistently speaks to men. It turns out that many others share my misgivings. We have found it useful and enlightening, therefore, during retreats, to discuss the drum factor for the benefit of those whose left brains are resisting.

Drummer boys

I see the drum beat as a male form of mantra. All the great world religions incorporate mantras. That is, people repeat something, usually words, as the men now do with the drums, monotonously, over and over, and this has been found to free the left brain from trying to conceptualize everything.

It is something like the gift of tongues for those who are charismatic; or the mesmeric power of the rosary. We also find that it is a great equalizer. One does not have to be a musician to play a drum. It allows everyone to enter into the creation of the rhythm without any expertise.

The organ most of us grew up with in church did not fall

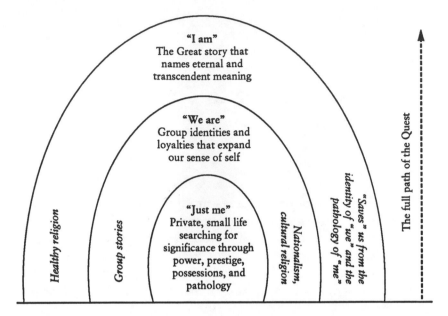

from heaven as God's sacred instrument. An examination of the history of culture will show the persistent sacred instrument is clearly the drum. It does not depend on one virtuoso performance. Rather, it is precisely an expression of community — all of us are drumming for the spirit, listening for the spirit, all of us are the celebrants.

The drum also validates the instinctual. It is an echo of the heartbeat, which is the first sound we hear, for nine months. There is, therefore, something primal and archetypal at work here, and the deep drum is connoting in our deep psyche something secure and warm — the womb.

There is a problem, however: Most of us have not been validated in our instinctual selves. We have been validated, if at all, only in our cerebral selves. Those of us raised within the church were, for the most part, warned to suppress the instinctual person, which was assumed to lead inevitably to various kinds of iniquity. This, we are now learning, was not the case at all.

Because we isolated and banished the instinctual, the level

of morality achieved in Western Christianity is often infantile. We are deprived of a fully human grasp of good and evil. Instead, we merely play with concepts. Finally it is time to go deeper than the conceptual. We must acquire a gut feeling for what is real and unreal, good and bad, authentic and inauthentic.

The hero is saying that your life is not just a personal matter. However incomprehensible it may seem to us Western individualists, the boundaries of our lives are bigger than ourselves. The "just me" self is not very interesting. The hero moves beyond "just me" to "we are," and finally to the biblical "I am."

The authentic hero is the one willing to set out on that larger quest for wider boundaries.

Ironically, the hero thinks he is embarking on something new. Every young man has that notion. It is sometimes called "wanderlust," or the desire for an almost geographical solution. There are no geographical solutions, but we tend to think there are.

Many people come to New Mexico, for example, for a geographical solution because we are supposed to be a spiritual state. The soul seems to be identified in the male by landscape and nature. The youth goes to a new space to see how the soul feels there. But the hero is not searching for something new, though he thinks he is. The discovery, usually in the middle of the journey, is rather that he is looking for something old that has been lost.

That is why connecting with the great myths of the ancestors, and connecting with nature and creation, is always crucial. Going out to seek something new, and finally rediscovering something old, is the reinstatement of the fallen world, of the universe, first of all within his own soul. This walking in what seems a circular journey represents a coming back to where he started and, as poet T. S. Eliot suggested, knowing the place for the first time.

Sometimes it is described as first naiveté, then complex consciousness, and then returning to second naiveté, and from the outside it looks like a return to simplicity, and it is.

Albert Einstein once said that as he looked for his theory of relativity, all he had beforehand was a predisposition, the conviction that whatever he would find would be *simple* and *beautiful*. This from, of all people, a scientist. In our day, clergy are becoming psychologists, while scientists are becoming mystics, much more open to mystical consciousness than many clergy. They have come to the limits and now are open to the awesome.

Great scientists, then, know the principle of uncertainty. It is the small-minded scientist who thinks it can all be explained rationally. Yet the unexplainable is mirrored in the smallest world of the atom and in the biggest world of the galaxy. The hero is asking not so much the how as the why of chaos. Why me? Why the brokenness and imperfection at the heart of so much beauty? We rail against it, we resist it. It shouldn't be this way, the soul wants to say.

The labyrinth

Western civilization was shaped by Greek, Roman, Jewish, and Christian stories. We see the Greek and Roman worlds most vividly in our poetry. These myths are at the heart of how Western people see themselves. The most significant, for our present purposes, is the myth of the labyrinth or maze.

When Achilles conquers Troy, he wears a breastplate with a labyrinth on it. It is a symbol of himself: His inner self, his gut, which is literally covered by the maze, will not be surprised by the mystery and complexity of things. Life is a labyrinth to go through, and if we follow it we find our own center.

Perseus attacks Medusa and the same image occurs. Now it is on his shield. Anyone who ever got a Medusa look from a woman would understand the Perseus story. Medusa looks at a man and he turns to stone, loses all his juices, his motivation and power. Man after man approaches Medusa and then freezes. It is the power of the feminine.

Robert Bly tells the story of a man going into the store and wanting to buy a green sweater. His wife says she likes the blue sweater better, and suddenly he likes the blue sweater. Unbelievable.

Women for the most part carry our feeling world. Our mothers told us how to feel. That is one of the great insights of the men's movement, that we got our rules for how to feel from women. This is not bad, but it is only half the truth: There is also a male way for feeling.

Medusa personifies the ability of the negative feminine to petrify whatever is male. Perseus, for defense, has a shield with another labyrinth painted on the front. To approach the negative woman, he has to hold in front of himself the shield depicting the complexity of life and he does not dare look at her. Only if he approaches with the shield between him and her can he get past the Medusa look and not turn to stone.

In Florence, Italy, there is a statue that men love — of a man holding the head of Medusa. Finally the man cut off the head of the negative woman. This is not anti-feminist. It is to recognize what myth has always needed to recognize: that there is a dark side and a light side to everything, and if we do not discover the dark side, and learn to put boundaries up against it, we will be destroyed by it.

The most famous labyrinth story is the one of the Minotaur, the beast that Theseus fights in the labyrinth. It is a good naming of the modern state of depression in which we do not know where the enemy is, what the path is, how to get in or out. And we do not know whether the Minotaur is within our own selves or separate from us.

Finally, Theseus does kill the Minotaur, but only after he has used a string to find his path. This string was given to him by a woman. The woman is symbol for the soul-wisdom that tells us how to make it through the maze.

Western civilization does not want to believe life is a labyrinth or maze. But in Chartres Cathedral in France one can see that Christianity once did understand the appropriateness of the myth. Right in the center aisle of the cathedral, directly before the altar, is a labyrinth. We cannot see the altar until we cope with the labyrinth. In the Middle Ages people would come to Mass early and "walk the labyrinth" as a devotion.

We, by contrast, have grown up with a post-Christian mythology of progress that is linear. We are indoctrinated into the progress myth, which says basically that the little boy, the male, must be taught that the goal in life is to get from here to there as quickly as possible, in lines as straight as possible. This may work in football but has nothing to do with the spiritual life.

The spiritual dynamic is two steps forward, then perhaps three back. The important thing is that the hero keep his eye on the path, and learn from the path. He sees that the three steps backward have as much to teach as those two forward. Perhaps more.

The success trap

So-called success is very insignificant in the spiritual journey. The nineteenth-century theologian Søren Kierkegaard wrote that in the West we are producing the tragic hero. Kierkegaard defined the tragic hero as the cultural hero of conformity. Whoever accepts the conventions for climbing the ladder, the progress myth of money and power, that is our tragic hero. Kierkegaard claims the male in the West is especially trapped in this syndrome between the ages of twenty and thirty-five. During those years, the man does what he is supposed to do. He is given the rules, and he pledges his allegiance.

Trouble is, young men do not know who they are at that stage. They know only what they are supposed to be, and the rules of the game. To rest in this mode constitutes the tragic hero of conformity. Kierkegaard carefully distinguishes this from the genuine knight of faith. He uses the Abraham story to exemplify the true knight of faith.

Abraham responded to a deeper truth, a subversive voice, as opposed to the conventional external wisdom that everyone else followed. He refused to ask any of the practical questions. His land, his wife, his children, his cattle, his fields, his reputation — he lost them all as God decreed: "Leave it all for a new land that I will show you" (Genesis 12:1).

There is not one pragmatic sound to God's voice. There is in Abraham's call not one sound that would make sense to a Western person. Yet, three of the great world religions — Islam, Judaism, Christianity — call Abraham father of their faith. He is the symbol, in one mythic story, for what faith means. He moved from security to insecurity, from having the answers to having no answers. He left all, as the voice taught, and heard that he would be given sons as numerous as the sands by the sea. He died not seeing the promise fulfilled, but putting his hope and identity in a different kind of success. That's the true knight of faith.

Mid-life is the usual final chance to choose for the true knight of faith. Normally, if we have not made any serious choices for freedom or truth, if we have not taken any great risks by the time we are fifty, we are too entrenched to make any more radical decisions. The marriage is formed, the children raised or almost, and everything is linked to the established myth.

To sell out now is scarcely possible. Few new questions are possible. The questions we ask and answer are the old ones. We are trapped.

But God can do it. I think that's why we must have a mid-life crisis — it is God shaking the tree one more time, and challenging: Will you give up the illusion? Will you stop just being what you think you are supposed to be? Who are you anyway?

The Grail myth

This sets the stage for the Grail myth. Middle age is when we start listening to the voices from other rooms and other spaces, instead of just the voices of ego-consciousness. For the young man to successfully build the tower, he must listen to ego and consciousness; he cannot allow the invasion of the unconscious. I am convinced — and the church does not seem to grasp this — that the rules are different for the first one third of life than for the next one third and finally for the last section.

We keep teaching people rules for the first one third and that's all. And suddenly they're sixty and those rules do not help anymore. In fact, after we build the tower, we must jump from it. The West teaches, to the contrary, that people must just keep on building the tower. More stones and more lifting, more effort, control, and accomplishment.

Discipline and order and law are necessary for an eighteen-year-old. He had better learn it: That's building the tower. Ego-morality, the world of logic and discipline, is the way to success in the system. You've got to do it at twenty-one — it's okay then. If you don't build the tower, you're in trouble; you will be seen as useless and shiftless, "drugs-sex-and-rock-and-roll"; you won't stand for anything.

First comes the law and then the spirit — John the Baptist before Jesus. And Jesus, by the way, never puts down the law — you've got to start with the law, or you don't start. It's the good and necessary "heroic instinct" in a young man.

When the eighteen-year-old has become sixty and is still putting all his energy into law and order and control, he's a stick-in-the-mud. There's no creativity, there's no freedom, no eros, no soul. We wouldn't follow such a man anywhere. He's got nothing to say, nothing that inspires or motivates others.

There is, in other words, a pattern to our male lives.

Priests know this from dealing with young males. Every

boy who comes in private for counseling is likely to be there about masturbation; there seems to be no other topic. But once we understand the tower, we can see that for young males that can be the first little victory. He needs to know he can say no to himself. Sometimes this drive is put into sports, or some other area where he can be strong. This is the beginning of the heroic instinct. He may not succeed, but it is important to be in that struggle. The young male has a deep need to triumph over the sensual self, over ego gratification. The tower is an ascent above the devouring but comforting "earth."

The tower is a way to remove himself from the feminine. The feminine is the world of feeling, nurture, warmth, and security. The male may easily be charmed and lured to stay in that environment indefinitely. This is why male initiation rites always taught the boy to separate from his mother. He is called by rituals of ancient culture to separate from what will pull him in, soften and seduce him.

In the great myths, the feminine is always the Siren. Odysseus must lash himself to the mast as the ship sails by the Sirens, that is, the women who, by their calls, draw all the men on to the rocks and kill them.

Then they must sail past the rocks of Scylla and Charybdis. Scylla is this lovely woman in a cave who looks rather attractive from the waist up. She, too, is calling the men. But as soon as they get close, she comes up a little higher out of the water, and there are six dog heads that come out of her midsection and chew the men up.

Charybdis, on the other side, is the feminine whirlpool that entices the male into comfort, pleasure, and self-concern.

The story of how Odysseus copes with these trials demonstrates how we must cut ourselves off from immediate gratification and temporary good feelings so we can get on with our journey. It is a harsh no to the false self. It does not have to be negative, but at its best is earnest, focused, and even a "sacred no."

The stuff women give us

It starts with Momma. I myself was my mother's favorite. I was allowed to be a little king. I had a younger sister and an older sister. My mother was a beautician, and all these little, blue-haired ladies would come to get their hair fixed and I grew up at their feet. They all thought I was so cute. (So I still expect women to think I'm cute!)

Because of this abundant contact with the feminine, I'm at home in the internal world of the anima. I can talk about spirituality non-stop. Where did I get that? The woman gives you that, gives you your internal world. I had so many loving women around me, I could live in the feminine with great self-confidence and ease.

But in the end that becomes the whirlpool that sucks us in, a whirlpool of thrashing around in our internal feelings. Too much subjectivity.

The male myths call us beyond the whirlpool, beyond the Sirens, past Scylla and Charybdis, to the journey, to the outer objective world. That, finally, is "king energy." Men who have king energy are secure in the world of tools, the land, their own bodies, finance and politics. It is a special kind of security one expects and needs from a father/king. He holds the "realm" together (*res* is the Latin for things, reality, what is).

If spirituality does not lead us to a recognizing of the Spirit in the concrete and the particular and the ordinary, I don't trust it. If you cannot find God there, you are going to be forever on a fruitless search for the esoteric (too much inner because the outer disappoints you).

Ultimately what we will find *out there* is how to see. We will then see that what we were seeking all along was back here in the ordinary world. When we achieve this, we are at home. Then we will know that the magical is happening right here. The *outward* signs are also, in the words of the catechism, "instituted by Christ to give grace." Spirituality is not about being "spiritual"!

A tower to jump from

The guide on this journey has two tasks to fulfill, which could be described by the titles "prophet" and "priest."

The prophet guides through the "path of the fall" (how to separate, fail, withdraw from the system). The priest guides us in the "path of the return" (how to see, what to see, where the sacred is to be found, union and desire).

First, the prophet must teach the would-be hero to enter the maze. We do not, today, have many who are willing and able to do this. We have, instead, slick televangelists who give us an answer without the labyrinth. They do an end-run around soul and around body. Just jump over — a non-stop flight — to spirit, and you have cheap, glib religion.

The first task is to tell the hero about the maze and give him the rules to enter it. This formation is done in the language of courage, of wisdom, of persistence, of patience — of starting with the tower but then recognizing we must let go of the tower, that it's time to jump off, or at least slowly descend.

The late Trappist monk Thomas Merton wrote of the people who climb to the top of the ladder and then ask in dismay, "Is that all there is?" And poet Robert Bly talks of all the men who climb the ladder and then find it's against the wrong wall.

The only point of the tower, and of the ladder, is to jump off it. But when you've invested thirty years building a really good tower, you're a good Catholic man, you've obeyed all the rules, and maybe you even have three vows, and you are so holy and secure — you don't want to jump off that tower.

To jump off: That's called faith. The rules change at that point. It's not law. It's paradox. It's mystery. It's darkness. It's freedom. It's ecstasy and it's agony. And we need a whole different set of rules at that point. Not ego morality but soul morality, which asks much more.

We in the church are not giving people these rules. We're mostly teaching people ego-morality of the first stage: law and discipline, black and white, in or out. The church has become an embarrassment in its unwillingness to recognize the real meaning of faith.

Mere credal religion or civil religion just does not give us access to the rich and revelatory unconscious. We will dive off the tower only if we have allowed grace to invade our consciousness, the unconscious to invade the conscious. We must take the lid off. That is why we talk about the instinctual and, if you will, the primitive, the primal.

I promise you, it's not going to lead us away from God; it's going to lead us to God, but it will often feel dangerous.

We're terribly afraid of taking the risk. This partially derives from filtering the Gospel through the Greek world, which was a head world, and the Roman world, which was an organization world. It wants control and order.

But if we rely on the props of Roman organization and Greek headiness, we will pretty much have taken the fire out of the belly of the Gospel.

Read how Jesus describes reality. Most of his examples are nature examples and relationship examples; he hardly ever quotes the scriptures. He says instead, "Look! Look at the sky. Look at the lilies of the field and you'll know what they're saying. Look at the sparrows, at the lady losing a dime." Understand how things work, the patterns that connect the nature of things.

He's a primitive teacher, in a way. He's not moving us into a conceptual world. We must go back to the world he showed us, and we must trust it.

Psychologist Carl Jung says it rather absolutely: Transformation happens only in the presence of images. Most religions since the beginning of time realized that transformation takes place in the presence of images, not in the presence of concepts. Ideas don't change people.

(Whatever concepts are presented here — and I give far too many concepts, because I'm a left-brained Westerner, too — are so that the reader will somehow dismantle them. I hope we can all move to a different level, where the images speak. And when the images are allowed to speak — when, for example, a person *personifies* some concept I have expressed — then you'll know my concept. Until you see a man who is a king, not until then do you understand a king. It may be that our words clear away some of the garbage so that we can know what to look for; words allow us, for example, to focus on why this man fascinates us, or why we wish we could be like him, or why we want to go with him on the journey. We want to go because now we know the journey is possible, the quest is real.)

Our job is, by our personhood and our words, to tell our brothers that the quest is real, that there is something more than winning in this tiny little fishbowl.

There are, then, two paths. There is the path of the fall. This is designed to lead people into the maze. It is, by the way, symbolized in Genesis by the fall. The individual must fall. We must teach the young, and give them the courage, and give them the net so that they can fall gracefully, so that they can enter into the Great Defeat. This is the same project as building the tower precisely so that we can fall off it.

The Twelve Step groups are doing that probably better than any other Christians right now: providing the net to allow people into the labyrinth of failure. This is much closer to Gospel spirituality than we find in the more fundamentalist-oriented institutional religions, which insist there is no labyrinth and that there is no need to fall.

Remember St. Paul in Romans 7:1–25: The law was given so you'd break it. In mythology, anywhere you find the prohibition, "don't do this," you can be sure they will do it. That's the point of the law — so they'll break it. And then experience the alienation, the loss, the loss of soul, the sense of separation from the great mystery, the great truth. This is the leaving of the garden, with angels at the gates with crossed swords. It is apparently necessary to experience alienation and aloneness. It is the prophet who leads us there — and then the priest teaches us the way of the return.

Panting and yearning

The soul pants and yearns. The Greeks called that *pothos* and *pathos* — yearning and feeling. Without pathos and pothos, there was no Greek tragedy. And in Greek tragedy the desired outcome was a cleansing of the soul — as you walk through that yearning you find out what you really desire. But we can't re-enter unless we're separated. And we must feel this separation. We must feel our sin, to use the Christian word. We must wake up some day with the realization, "I'm a dumb ass." Sick and tired of being sick and tired.

Normally the quest begins with a pronounced feeling that we are dying, that we're losing it, that life isn't making sense. Those glittering with success, with wonderful marriages, with all the toys: They have a problem. Such people are not going to go anywhere. They think they have already arrived. That's called inflation.

There is a dance with inflation, where you experience the Grail and then you lose it and then you long for it and come back in at a deeper level. And then you will lose it again, I promise you: You cannot keep the law, and you cannot stay on the honeymoon.

In the beginning of the myth the Grail is veiled, only partially seen, but enough to realize what it is. This is the first religious experience of a young man — just enough to know the real, to know there is something more, something even eternal.

The second path is called the path of the return. It's how to escape from the labyrinth when you're sick and tired of being sick and tired; when you know your life is phony and hypocritical and you're ashamed to share your true feelings and thoughts with anyone; when you hate the self and hate the soul. How to escape? "How to be at-one again?" is the priestly question.

The answers are faith, love, forgiveness, freedom, hope, desire, reconciliation with the dark side, with the sin of others and even the sin of the world.

But in the church we are making the mistake of teaching people the language of return before we have taught them the language of the fall. We must get them into the maze, into the mystery, into leaving the garden and disobeying Daddy. That's why the young boy rebels — he has to.

We have all met those stuffy old Catholics who still believe the pope's every word is infallible — they're so good but so useless, there's nothing there. It's not their fault: No one ever told them they could walk the journey, or take risks, because the love they had heard about wasn't that secure, the Father apparently not father enough.

There usually has to be some loss of faith in the established certitudes, all the things we pledged allegiance to. This is a scary course. If you want to look good in Daddy's eyes and Mommy's eyes, you can look good, and be good, but no one will ever follow you, no souls saved in your wake, nothing will be transformed (including yourself). This is a sterile, literalized, basically secularized world that tries to present itself as faith. The best disguise for faith I can think of is called religion.

Just look at Jesus. You know what killed Jesus? Conventional wisdom. It wasn't evil people. Scholars now say that Judaic religion was never lived better than at the time of Jesus. They were true to the law, "the law of holiness," of Leviticus 17–27. The scribes, Pharisees, and lawyers whom we try to paint as bad people were in fact good people — according to conventional wisdom. They were following the rules.

Most people won't set out on the search unless sometime, however briefly, the Grail was unveiled for them. It may have been when they were four years old, and suddenly they knew. I think of it lately as the clap of the Zen master's hand — clap! — it can be that quick, and you know it's radically okay. Or maybe it was at fourteen, when you first fell in love with someone. Those lucky enough to experience the unveiling of the Grail know it's okay to stay in the maze.

Sadly, in our day, the warriors and lovers are going nowhere with their warrior energy. Violent young men are aimless in their destruction. And the lovers have become mostly addicts. And perhaps it's inevitable: The warriors and lovers are going to lose the battle when there are not enough kings or magicians. And we are not producing magicians or kings. There are no fathers to hold the net together, to say, "Son, this is going to work and that isn't."

And the good king will no doubt add, "Go ahead and make your mistake, I give you permission to make it, and I'll be here to accept you back when you blow it, and I'm telling you now so that later you'll remember that I told you."

A chance to blow it

And the boy will remember. But first he probably has to go and make the mistake. And the good father is the one who can allow him to make it.

I had a number of wonderful father figures in my life. One was Cardinal Joseph Bernardin of Chicago. When he was archbishop of Cincinnati, he would occasionally call me in and show me the sheaf of complaints about me. I expected the worst. But he said: I had my theologian look at all these, and we trust you. I was only twenty-eight, a little would-be warrior, a would-be magician. But he gave me the space. He held the net for me. He'd say, "You and I, keep in touch."

I wanted to live up to that love and trust. I didn't want to embarrass him. He gave me grandfather energy. He taught me how to accept my own father energy. That's what a king does for the warriors. Wise people say one can't be a king, with full access to the king energy, before one is fifty. By that time one has seen the patterns enough, has been through the labyrinth enough, so that one can say it's probably necessary for the young warrior to go down that road.

Sin is not the worst thing in the world. On Holy Saturday we call it *felix culpa,* happy fault. That doesn't mean it's not sin, doesn't mean you won't pay for it. You do evil and — the inexorable wheel — it has to be undone; it's a law of nature.

But we don't have kings. And when we don't, the dark warriors and immature heroes dominate.

The heroic rules apply only at the beginning. In the middle you're not a hero. You feel like you're a dumb ass in the middle. It feels good at twenty-five to be a hero, conquering this and that, building the tower. But heroism doesn't work. Finally, our hero is naked, bleeding, condemned, rejected. The image of Jesus in his most important moment is not that of a hero. He looks like a loser, a victim. Unless you're willing to look like a bad boy, you won't be a hero. If you keep needing to look like a good boy — which is what we Ones on the enneagram do — you'll never learn.

Whom does the Grail serve? In the beginning, it's serving just you. To follow the rules, to please the big daddies and mammas makes you feel good. It's not love of God; it's love of self, love of your own reputation or power. Who wouldn't want to be a hero? It works in the system.

Sanctity is something much bigger than heroism — where you live in the darkness and the agony of faith, and you don't know you're right, and the authorities might even be criticizing you.

Body, soul, and spirit

Biblical anthropology was divided three ways. In the Old Testament the human person was divided into body, soul, and spirit. The only time we have it clearly defined is in the last paragraph of Paul's first letter to the Thessalonians: "May God make you whole in body, soul, and spirit."

But by the time he gets to Romans and Galatians, Paul changes the whole paradigm to flesh and spirit, and that's the one we, for the most part, grew up with — spirit being good and flesh bad, which was terribly unfair.

But Paul was trying to make a different point: Flesh was

what was trapped in the momentary, and spirit was open to the transcendent and the totality and the universal.

If we are not open to the unconscious, we are not open to the totality, and therefore usually not very open to God. Ego consciousness is just open to what *I* know (which is usually what I *want* to know). That means putting the lid on the unconscious, because the unconscious will be passionate, sexual, fiery, scary, wonderful, angry — all the things I don't want to feel because I might stop going to church. (The best Catholics I know usually left the church for a while, and then they returned, and when they did they knew what it's really about: It's a lot more relativized and not an idolatrous religion anymore. I wonder sometimes if it's not necessary to leave for a while.)

The spirit part of the person is that which keeps us open to the further and transcendent and beyond, which we would finally call God. Spirit in you seeks Spirit in God.

"Soul" is the word that got confused. The word is *psyche* in Greek. (The original word *psyche* means butterfly, they say. That's how ephemeral and hard it is to get a hold of soul.)

In practically every Western church, soul was understood to be that eternal part of us that goes either to heaven or hell. And the job of priests was to save that soul.

That, however, was not the historic meaning of soul. The historic soul was, rather, that part of us which has to do with depth. It might help to depict it in spatial images. Picture spirit as a vertical image going up to the transcendent. Soul goes down into the depths of things, into the meaning of things, into the unconscious and symbolism of things. It's what happens in dreams, and in mythology, and in story and poetry — that's all the world of soul.

The reason, they say, the Irish are so good at blarney is because Celtic religion, before St. Patrick got a hold of the natives, was all songs and poems. Religion at its best was always the singing of songs and expressing the mystery of things — the assumption being that if we go down and open up this great space within us, there will be room for the transcendent, room for Spirit.

My assumption is that if you don't do soul work there is no room for Spirit. You'll just be Catholic and who cares? Merely credal religion does not give us access to transcendence and with it the bounty of reconciliation and healing.

Women know body better

It is our sisters who are rediscovering the mystery and power of the body. Women are more in touch, so to speak, with the body. Why? Menstruation? Childbirth? In most cultures women never had initiation rites. They didn't need them, because their initiation rite was already in their body. And their body told them life is painful. Their ejaculation — of a child from their body — is, unlike that of men, a painful experience.

We men do not understand the pain of birthing, of bringing things to life. The woman *understands* in her body, and this is where we have to learn from the feminists. The Greek myths make the male Sky Father, counterpart of Earth Mother. We need to pull him back to earth. It's the movement of the incarnation: that God in Jesus became flesh and in doing so proclaimed that flesh is okay.

Recall the occasion when Jesus washed the feet of his brothers. Now recall where he learned this. A woman came into a room filled with men. One can imagine the snickers. There was no conceptual theology here, no sermons — not logos but eros. Logos is conceptual and verbal clarification, and that's the male way; we like words. (Yet, we like to drum too, and maybe that's because even we get tired of words. Maybe because the words have led us nowhere.)

So the woman comes in. She gets down — I know this is a gesture that culturally may be lost on us, so we don't fully understand the relationship or the impact — and washes his feet with her tears and dries them with her hair. And Jesus

---

Ways of Knowing

Intellectual: Reason, logic, and formal education's response to truth. Preferred form of Western people.

Volitional: When truth is known by choices and commitments we make. Tied to time, memory, struggle of ongoing, refined decisions.

Emotional: When the great emotions (anger, fear, hatred, desire, ecstasy, grief) are able to open us to truth. Eventually necessary to fully "know." Underplayed by intellectuals.

Bodily/sensory: When the actions and movements and five senses of the body themselves teach us truth. Despite supposed sacramentalism of the church, it has deeply mistrusted "corporeal theology."

Imaginative: When the truth of the larger unconscious is known, usually through pictures, stories, dreams, images, and fantasies. The way of myth that is used in this book, for example. Awakening the archetypes that are operating unconsciously anyway. Gives coherence to life and knowledge. "Ego-consciousness" resists its scary power.

Aesthetic: When matter and form come together to create the beauty or ugliness of truth. Most attractive, but often least converting. The dilettante, politically correct; or truly great artist.

Epiphanic: The peak experiences and breakthrough moments that reveal Big Truth. "The Grail experience," as here described. Cannot be orchestrated or manufactured. Always grace! Ironically, church tends to mistrust or be threatened by such epiphanies, and sometimes for good reasons. Relativizes all other forms of knowing and all other systems. Needs a good lover to experience it, a good warrior to not indulge it, a good magician to learn what it is really saying and what it is not saying, and a good king to hold it together in "real-ity."

---

says: This will be remembered to the end of time, and when it is remembered the world will remember her (Matthew 26:13). The line is almost comparable in its solemnity to "Do this in remembrance of me." We did the one in memory of him; we never did the other in remembrance of her.

True, for some centuries washing the feet was considered a sacrament, but throughout most of the church we forgot that one very early. Some bishops still won't let women have their feet washed liturgically. The culture has made it embarrassing for men to do so.

This is body theology. The body doesn't lie. So some of us are still carrying our childhood wounds on our back, and in our ulcers. Meanwhile, our church wants to bypass the body and get into safe, heady, orthodox religion. When will the hierarchical and teaching church understand that there are many ways of knowing? Intellectual knowing is the least converting and compelling, and yet it is the one we demand of believers. It is bodily, imaginative, and epiphanic knowing that changes lives. Great Catholicism always understands the many ways of knowing.

But what are all those orthodox people doing for the world? If they don't know how to listen to their body, they don't know how to listen to their soul. So, finally, the world is not listening to them. Consequently, the credibility of the church seems, year by year, to be less and less. And this is because, ultimately, it is not giving its members access to God, to the transcendent, to the truth.

We need to give ourselves permission to do some body work as well as some soul work, and we need to trust that work: that it will not lead us away from God but will in fact widen and deepen the path toward full transformation in Christ — the enfleshed one.

Chapter 3

The separation and departure _____

One thing many people, especially women, dislike about men is that they are often unwilling talkers. Indeed, one of the reasons men like to drum is the fact that it allows them to avoid being verbal. The most common complaint I hear from wives is that their men do not want to talk.

This complaint is so commonplace that there must be something in the male makeup that abhors talk, that instead prefers to go inward and ponder. And drumming provides a perfect excuse to be alone with our feelings and thoughts. This seems a plausible explanation why, in culture after culture, men gather around campfires and drum. They relate better shoulder to shoulder than jaw to jaw, talking.

Guys will stick together in the trenches, shoulder to shoulder. In a common action men feel a kind of union, a loyalty and caring, a bonding. We are not competitive anymore. We are drumming for the same battle, the same issues. We may not be sure what the issue is, but we don't need to know. The soul does not have to be understood.

We used to talk about the work of the priest as *cura animarum*, the care of souls. This may be what we're trying to do in the men's movement. Just silently mulling over things. Giving ourselves permission to feel a broken heart, or anger or desire, is maybe what a ritual like this is about. I don't know for sure. But we don't need to understand everything we do. That's part of the myth of rationalism, that everything has to be understood. Doing some things faithfully and even monotonously is also a way of knowing.

Good ways not to understand reality

In mythology there is no desire or effort to explain reality. It is, rather, an experience of reality. Most of us live too exclusively in our heads, especially those who are overeducated. Until we get the meaning, we don't know how to release ourselves to things. This betrays a lack of faith. And a hankering for control. "I want control and I will not submit to anything I don't understand — I will not 'stand under' it."

To stand under it means to give ourselves to the experience and let *it* teach us. The instinctual world knows that, but most of us don't experience our experiences. That's why we are not converted men and not a converted culture — we have not found ways to experience our experiences.

There was no need for the Mass to be translated into English. We could have sat there before the Latin Mass and listened to the Gregorian chant and experienced our experiences. That's pretty much the nature of universal religion. The soul mediates, it is almost like a bridge across the river between the conscious and unconscious. The soul carries the images across. It mediates between the body and the spirit.

What we are now trying to open up is precisely that mediation point. True religion leads us to the great feelings, not the little ones. The great ones are those we would die for, the ones we would change our lives for. The great desire. The great compassion. The great anger. The great loyalty. The great communion. Those feelings come out of the great sea of the unconscious. That whole other self that we fear, and are afraid to know.

We can't risk the invasion of our unconscious until we have a clear sense of identity, an appropriate sense of our own and others' boundaries, and some sense of the sacred or absolute. There are, in fact, many such immature people, who allow the invasion of the unconscious but have no ego-boundaries, no sense of their identity. They're all over the place and therefore they're nowhere. This is unfortunately the norm rather than the exception in our society today.

The permissive society refuses to offer the young man any boundaries that say no. The market culture sees no need for the sacred when all things are merely bought and sold for a price. Cheap liberalism always avoids commitment, and therefore identity. The church, in gross overreaction, throws out a string of no's, offers the sentimental as a substitute for the scary sacred, and calls for commitment to church identity instead of faith and discipleship. It won't work.

Old talk and the ineffable

Heinrich Zimmer said, "The best things cannot be talked about. The second-best things are usually misunderstood." The second-best things are what we're trying to explore here. It is the world of images, metaphors, symbols, stories, and myths. They're usually misunderstood in our logical, material world. And because we're tired of being misunderstood, tired of people calling us heretics or eccentrics or New Age practitioners, we just don't talk about such things. Who wants to be misunderstood all the time?

The second-best things are those that point toward the first best (which can't be talked about!). All religion is metaphor. This is reflected in the first and second commandments. There is only one God, and don't try to carve images of this God, because all the images are metaphors, approximations at best, fingers pointing to the moon. And, as we know, we tend to fight about the fingers instead of looking at the moon. Everybody wants the one, holy, catholic, apostolic finger. Then we fight over who has the true finger. Does your finger save, or does mine? Neither. Only God names and liberates.

So much religious idolatry happens in protecting the metaphors, as if they were the end product. We burned people at the stake because they didn't accept the right metaphor. We exclude people from the universal table fellowship Jesus proclaimed because they don't say it the way we do. When religion confuses the metaphor with the real thing, it makes the wonderful process of transformation into something mechanical. The mysterious and personal God is transmuted into a vending machine, and we are pushing the buttons.

So we spend most of our lives talking about the third best things. The safe, containable, controllable, measurable, legalized things. Sports, weather, and what the neighbors are doing.

What I hope we're daring to do as we enter into the Grail myth is to talk about the second-best things — the great stories, the fingers pointing to the mystery of Spirit.

It is said that Homer wrote the *Illiad* and *Odyssey*, but it is probably more accurate to say he reworked the collected stories of many tribes, stories that had been evolving since our earliest ancestors sat around a fire to amuse or educate or scare each other with yarns. If a story endures, we can be sure it is naming something in the unconscious. It would not last if it were not jerking something inside us. That is the power of good pictures, too. We should each find for ourselves an appropriate picture, one that breaks the heart, and then ask why.

Of all the myths of Western civilization as we know them up to that time, Homer's were the myths that named the male journey, in the eighth century B.C.E. Away from Ithaca and back to Ithaca again. And all the trials in between. Then, in the twelfth and thirteenth centuries C.E., the pattern was repeated. If there is any myth after Homer that names the journey of the male, Western, Christian soul, it is the myth of the Holy Grail. It emerged in the late twelfth century and developed in the thirteenth and fourteenth centuries in many different forms. The Germans and French each developed their own versions. Finally it evolved into the Arthurian legend among the English. But it was everywhere among the European nations, and it was elaborated as it spread. People would drop and add things until it finally came to be known as the quest for the Holy Grail.

The word "Grail" itself may have come from the Spanish

for "royal blood" — the myth of the holy or divine blood (*sangre real; san graal*). It finally became Christianized as the search for the cup used by Jesus at the Last Supper.

Jung wrote at length about the symbolism of blood in culture after culture. The drinking of the blood is probably the most primal, universal symbol of getting the essence of the other person. Getting the energy and power of the other. This helps explain the power and the primitiveness of the Christian Eucharist. This is what we are building on. But unfortunately we have diluted the concept and made it an antiseptic caricature of the original on our lace-covered altars. Thus the bloody, gutsy image of drinking the blood of the hero has in great part been lost even on Christians who do it every day.

Where the Grail legend grew

We're going back to this myth that grew, at least in part, out of our understanding of the Eucharist. The hero, in some versions, was a man named Parsifal (not surprisingly, the spelling of his and other names differed from country to country). In Old English the name means the Perfect Fool.

It is not clear whether that name refers to the beginning or the end of the journey. In the myth, one is supposed to begin with naiveté, then walk through the complexity and paradoxes of the labyrinth, and return at the end in second naiveté. At the end point of the journey the hero is presented as the perfect fool, the holy fool, like St. Francis. The one who goes for broke. The one who knows already the meaning of the rules, so he does not have to obey the rules anymore.

It is characteristic of how these myths set common sense on its head that a name such as the Perfect Fool should be a badge of distinction. Some try to interpret it through the French and say it means "pierced through the middle." Even that would be a lovely interpretation of the name. The one who is defeated. The one with the broken heart. The Catholic tradition that generated all those pictures of the bleeding sacred heart of Jesus seems to us rather sentimental, but it is archetypal. It is, finally, what everybody experiences on the journey. The wounded heart pierced through the middle.

Most versions of the legend begin with a wasteland kingdom. It is being ruled over, though barely ruled, by one called the Fisher King. He is wounded. The wound seems to be in the groin. The implication seems to be a wound in sexuality or in fertility. He is not a fertile king. Therefore, the whole kingdom is not fertile. The crops are dying, the monasteries are empty, the people are depressed. All the king can do, because his wound refuses to heal, is fish all day — that is why he is called the Fisher King. The name obviously has Christ connotations too, the "fisher of men."

All the citizens know that as long as the king is sick, the kingdom is going to be sick. Thus, we have the wounded father figure, the one holding the system together. The system is sick at the top. But, interestingly, he is fishing. Water invariably symbolizes the great universal unconscious. We don't know what is under the water. This was literally true before modern submarines and such. What is the great mystery down there? The sea is the natural image of the vast unconscious. I think this is the reason we can sit by the ocean for hours and watch it in fascination. Waiting for the gift from the sea, waiting for something to show itself. Fishing is the obviously appropriate symbol of dipping down into one's own unconscious.

In most mythologies the sea is described as wine-blood in color. Many researchers think the human eye could not see blue until the last several thousand years. In fact, the word "blue" is not to be found in any ancient literature.

Bread and fish tradition

The best scholarship says Jesus celebrated two traditions of fellowship meals: the bread and wine and the bread and fish.

We see the fish theme after the resurrection; we meet it in the story of the multiplication of loaves and fishes. It has even become the Christian logo, especially among crypto-Christians. The bread and fish tradition was a separate kind of ritual meal: It always has surplus as a characteristic. It is what we call potluck: Everybody comes together, shares, and there is always plenty left over for the poor.

It is very interesting that the bread and wine tradition continued and the bread and fish motif, which had more economic and practical implications, was lost. Paul was struggling with it in Corinthians, when people were bringing the food and losing the sense of the agape meal that has plenty left over for the poor.

So maybe the Fisher King is fishing for the Christ symbol in the great unconscious, probably searching for his own soul, for the great fish at the heart of European Christian civilization, for the practical meaning of the Gospel. Surely it means all of these.

We have a wasteland, a non-father, a non-king, a wounded king, eternally wounded and unable to be healed. He does not seem to be making any effort to get healed, except for throwing the hook into the sea.

Enter Parsifal

Into this story comes the perfect fool, Parsifal. Let us chart his life. First of all, perhaps not surprisingly, he is fatherless.

We live in a world without the father. Already in the twelfth century, the hero was personified that way — one who has no father. His father and his brothers were knights killed in battle. His mother tells him about father and brothers, but he has no immediate experience of masculinity, of maleness. His whole world is communicated to him through his mother. The stories usually say he is of royal lineage. All heroic stories are that way: All the heroes are noble. Christianity finally turned that around. The old lives of the saints were more likely to say they were born of pious and humble parents. One way to tell the pagan myths, which are more instinctual and gutsy, is the fact that the hero is of royal lineage.

People are to some degree aware they come from greatness, from God. As Wordsworth would say, "trailing clouds of glory." In fact, that, to me, is the meaning of the word "glory." When you are in glory, you recognize your origins, the heart of you is something beyond you, something greater than you. You are of royal ancestry. That, finally, is what all believers hope to discover: where they came from, who they are, who they were before they had a human face, before they did anything right or wrong.

The purpose of baptism is to wash away the illusion that we are merely sons of this earth. We have a divine origin. We came from God. The spiritual journey is about discovering the beginning. Not earning or creating it — just discovering who we already are. Jesus said, "Your names are written in heaven." We do not, therefore, have to write them there, since they are already there. Our destiny is to return where we began. That is the hero's journey — in the heavenly transcendent realm now.

Religion is always coming to that conclusion: that we have a divine origin. God does not make junk. We are not a mass of protoplasm that spontaneously happened. We are the choice of God.

So Parsifal has a royal lineage. His mother tells him so, and he believes it. Every mother tells her son how great he is, that in some sense he is royal.

Furthermore, besides being royal and without father, Parsifal is growing up in the woods, in nature. Very seldom are heroes found in the cities. This is the instinctual aspect of the hero, the nature collective.

The word "wilderness" acquired a special significance in the frontier myth here in America. In the eighteenth and nineteenth centuries, the ideal was so-called civilization, and "wilderness" became a bad word. This practically turned all mythology on its head. Previously, all mythologies idealized the wilderness. Or wildness. That's where the soul is discovered — in the wild. We have created a civilization that idealizes civilization and runs away from wilderness. Or we try to tame the wilderness, the wildness.

Not only have we tamed the wilderness, we have tamed the soul. Once we're tame, the only animal we deem appropriate is the domestic animal. I'm convinced that animals mirror back to us the essential parts of our soul. It's no accident that every men's group wants to name itself after some animal. Even the Cub Scouts — the Hawk Patrol, the Eagle Patrol.

The experience of animals, especially when they look at us, is almost numinous. The world beyond the human somehow is in communication with us. Jung said that "when religion stops talking about animals, it will be all downhill." I often thought that sounded a bit pagan, but then, not long ago, I was giving a retreat in Assisi, and I went to the old cathedral of San Rufino, which would have been there when St. Francis lived. On the front of this early medieval cathedral there is one picture of Christ right above the main portal, but the entire rest of the front of the cathedral is decorated with animals.

Today, some people would say, "Oh, my God, it's an occult church, it's New Age, it's pagan. Instead, it tells us that eleventh- and twelfth-century Italian Christians were still in touch with their ground, with their instinctual selves. Their religion was not all up in the sky or in the head. Western civilization has practically destroyed the woods. We did not respect the woods. But we idealized civilization, an anthropocentric world, our world, where we could make money, rather than a world in which we could see and understand our soul. And see it mirrored in the rhythms of the seasons, or in nightfall, or in the iconography of animals.

The longer I was in the hermitage, the fewer books I needed. And even fewer ideas. It was all there — the Bible of nature. It was the only time in my life I was awakened by moonrise. This sensation is so wonderful, it must realign us with something we need deep down. Not having TV or radio or other artificial sounds was delightful. I wrote back and told my friends I felt my ears were as wide as my shoulders, my eyes as wide as my head. In our regular lives, our eyes and ears numb out because there is nothing worth seeing or hearing. The wilderness, by contrast, feels like a purification and an ecstasy of knowing. Epiphanic knowledge.

What's in a name?

Because he is raised only by his mother, in the first half of most versions of the myth Parsifal does not know his real name, only what his mother calls him, namely, "Dear Boy" or "Beautiful Son." When he first meets knights on the road and they ask him his name, he replies with the only name he has heard, Dear Boy or Beautiful Son.

We tend to know our inner glory and find our inner imagination (soul) from the loving gaze of the feminine. We tend to go to the outer world to find male approval and verification of the inner glory (body or spirit).

What he has not heard, of course, is what his father called him, since he does not have a father. That leaves him waiting for a name, the external validation of his inner glory.

At a certain point he starts insisting to his mother that he wants to leave home. She, of course, fights him. She gives the usual reasons: She needs him to take care of the house. But he is adamant. Every boy knows he has to leave home. He is driven to discover the great unconscious, the eternal feminine, the anima. His mother gave him hints, or promises. In a certain sense that's the first Grail image: his mother's love, the first love he experienced from the feminine.

Many men are wounded with the father wound. But a deeper wound, a harder one to heal, is that of the man who never experienced his mother. Apparently, for most of us, that's the first imprinting — when the mother looks upon us with utter delight, just thinking we're the cutest things in the world. For the rest of our lives we long to see that again. To have someone delight in us and call us dear boy, beautiful son. That, more or less, is what Jesus hears repeated in the desert. Hears it from his Father. The objective of the whole mythic journey is to have that first promise given by the mother echoed and renewed by the Father. Mother love is unearned grace. Father love is in a good and real sense "worked for."

In almost all mythology, the cup is a feminine symbol, a vaginal symbol, the great opening the man is always seeking, someplace where he can again be contained and held. The scariest place in the world and the most wonderful place in the world. It harks back to the eternal yearning for the mother. It is no surprise that we named most of the eight hundred cathedrals in France Notre Dame. Because our religion was so patriarchal, we made Mary, for all practical purposes, into a god. We needed the feminine face of God: pure grace.

The more macho a culture, the more the men will worship Mary. The more cold and distant the Father is, the more this fascination with the woman. Somehow we can trust Mary. In Ohio we used to have "Bathtub Marys." Folks would take an old bathtub, half-bury it spigot-end-down in the front yard, and make a little shrine out of it. People would not reproduce a statue that frequently unless it were archetypal. The statue of Mary is the woman with her arms outstretched, what every little boy saw when he came running across the room: "Come, Johnny, come to Mommy, I'll take care of you."

We're all waiting for this eternal great-breasted mother in the sky who will say, "Come to me. I'll take care of you." It makes good sense. One wonders how Protestantism got along without her. I once mentioned this to a group of Protestant ministers, and one of them suggested that they created instead a blond-haired, blue-eyed Jesus who is sweet and sentimental enough for the purpose. That's it, the sentimental Jesus of evangelicalism. None of the male demanding qualities, just all sweet.

This shows how the soul will find its truth. We can have all the orthodox theologies we want in our heads, but down below instinct wins anyway. We find what we need in order to break through. And what we needed was a woman side of God.

Much of what the nuns taught us was terrible theology. Most were Irish girls who became nuns and came to America to teach us bratty kids. But psychologically they were geniuses. Here's how Sister Ephraim conned us into goodness: "Say your rosary every day and that's the way you'll get to heaven."

When you get to heaven, this thesis went, St. Peter will be standing at the gate. (A man, of course.) You'll look through the gate, and there will be Jesus. (Another man.) If you look beyond Jesus, way back will be a big throne and on it God the Father with a big white beard. Three men between you and paradise. Formidable.

"But I'll show you the way to get in," Sister Ephraim said. Go around to the back door of heaven, she said. How do you find the back door? I don't know, but we were little fifth graders and we knew Ephraim would not lie to us, so there had to be a way to the back door of heaven.

"Now, if you have said your rosary all your life, you will recognize the way in," she went on, "because Mary will be standing at the back window of heaven with her rosary out the window. She'll pull you up into heaven for all eternity." We felt so excited. We knew the way now. Dubious theology, magnificent psychology.

Ephraim knew what most of us have also discovered: Mom will let us off the hook; Mom will not enforce the law, Mom loves us too much; Mom will let us through. The eternal feminine. The great breasts will always be there to feed us. That's the archetype. There's no point in continuing to call it lust, although it's that, too. We had better find out why it is so good that it fascinates men to such a degree that they would give up kingdoms for it.

When we were young Franciscans, we told our student master our idea of heaven was sex and hamburgers. Surely the first level of moral development! He was such a good man. He said, "You'll get it, then. That's what heaven will be." Sex and hamburgers.

This great cup, the great female mystery, the great open sea the man is always setting sail on to find his soul, is something positive. It is the yearning that feeds a man's wanderlust, urges him on the journey. He has seen enough of the cup to know there is a Holy Grail. There are many false Grails. And many lesser Grails, not necessarily bad, but what keeps a man going is the image of the perfect woman, the perfect soul. The perfect love. It is, finally, the search for God. The one who will finally name and satisfy my soul. The one who will accept my truth exactly as I speak it. One who will throw all my sins behind his or her back.

There is also a negative side to the feminine. It, also, must be named and guarded against. In mythology we also find Scylla and Charybdis. And there is Circe, who turns Ulysses and all his men into pigs. She gets them to love her and then gets them to move to the lowest level of their consciousness. Not to build a tower is to live instead at the level of the merely instinctual. Drugs and sex and rock and roll.

When the gods were women

Thus the bad news is that it is easy to regress into unconsciousness, which is really non-consciousness. That's what drinking is. That's what drugs are. What all addiction is. It's not increased consciousness, it's decreased consciousness. We don't want to feel our feelings. We don't want to know our thoughts, don't want to feel our pain, so we pick some artificial way to hide from these.

The negative side of the feminine is to want the breast

right away. It's the need for instant gratification. I'm not going to bother to build the tower. I won't say no to myself. It's that common cliché: pleasing ourselves. The false feminine pulls us into this.

Historians of religion figure that earth's earlier religions were goddess religions. There is compelling evidence that for centuries most cultures worshipped feminine gods — goddesses.

Our early ancestors, innocent of biology, saw the little child come out of the body of the woman. They did not know the connection between intercourse, conception, and birth, so obviously the woman played a star role in begetting new life. It was a short leap from there to imagining the image of God as a woman. The nurturing one with the big breasts. A totally new life came out of her body. She is clearly the god image.

It is not clear what men were for in that scenario. The people did not know we men had anything to do with the birth of a child. So we got into hunting and drumming and dancing   largely a ritual world. Men were the ritualists. Which is probably why priesthood was largely male, serving the goddesses.

With the rise of Judaism came the movement into patriarchal religion. Belief then turned to a male God. This trend continued. We all grew up with pictures of God as a man. There is a tendency today to see this as a regression.

When we had goddess-centered religion — the legend goes — we had fertility, we had joy, we were happier in a pastoral world dominated by images of fruits and vegetables and fields. It is said that the Irish, before they would plant their crops, would all make love in the fields at night. It's a magnificent scenario: Make love in the fields and the next day plant the seeds. Apparently most people did it. The symbolism is obvious. The fertility of the one increased the fertility of the other. There was no guilt or shame, or any reason for guilt or shame.

But it is also fair to say — and I don't think most feminists bring this up — that the religion of the goddess did not tend to produce a people with *outer confidence,* with what we finally call civilization. Civilization does not emerge until people have a sense of confidence in their own selfhood, apart from the great collective unconscious of feeling. When we started moving toward individuation, that was a movement into the masculine. The masculine is spirit, mind, logos. The feminine is earth, body, pleasure. Both have half the truth. Everything belongs.

But we had to move into patriarchal religion to get away from the merely instinctual, the merely pleasure-oriented. Admittedly, we overreacted. "Pleasure" and "body" and "joy" became bad words, and "earth" became a bad word. The whole new thrust was away from the earth, up to the sky. Build the tower. Because we became ashamed of the earth, ashamed of the wilderness, ashamed of the body, ashamed of blood, of sexuality, of menstruation.

In the Jewish religion it took three weeks to get purified after menstruation. Under such a regime, some women got into the temple only one or two days a month after being purified before the next menstruation was upon them. All because the show of blood was considered unworthy as society became more hygienic and unreal.

We are products of that period. We still experience the patriarchal reaction to centuries and centuries of goddess religion. So the world we grew up in was a father-centered religion, where the emphasis is law, structure, organization, obedience, loyalty. All these are virtues and it serves no purpose to put them down. But they are only half the truth. The rise in feminist consciousness is not likely to go away. Human consciousness has come to this point, and no pope or anyone else is going to put it back in the bottle. We are ready for the sacred marriage of mature femininity and mature masculinity.

The feminists have come to an awareness that is by and large true. Now our job is to find what is true in both. We need to mend the breach: What is true in masculine power, and building the tower, and spirit, and what's good about feminine instinct, and body, and intuition, and earth. We would never have raped the earth the way this century has raped the earth if we had a stronger feminine soul.

One reason the Native Americans of North America are so admired is because they seem to have achieved, like few other peoples, a beautiful balance of both. By and large the Great Spirit was thought of as masculine but entirely in a feminine way that respected and loved the earth. Even the pope, when he came to Phoenix, made a statement that continues to shock people — especially coming from this pope: There is nothing in the religions of North American Native Indians that is incompatible with Christianity. Extraordinary!

The peoples of this continent achieved a very high level of spirituality. It was not based on any killing of animals or peoples, as so many religions in other parts of the world were. It was not based on abuse or destruction, but always on enhancement and idealization and union.

Those of us who came here from outside, we colonists, we children of Europeans ought to remember this earth is still their earth, and their spirituality still shines here. They fascinate us precisely because their spirit is still amid these rocks and hills and fields, as it was for centuries. We tried to destroy their mythology. And now here we are, trying to put theirs and ours together. That, by the way, is something Catholicism always did well. It integrated the old religions of Europe with the revelation that came from Jesus and the Gospel. A Lutheran minister in Germany told me that "Catholics are still in touch with their pagan roots, whereas we Protestants are all in the head." He felt that was why Catholicism has such an amazing ability to transform and renew itself.

The devouring mother

It is important to acknowledge this history, including what's good about the feminine. But we must also recognize that the feminine has a dark side. In mythology we always had what the fairy tales called the wicked stepmother. She had many names: the devouring mother, the witch, Astarte, Ishtar, Kali. Very often, in those stories, the negative feminine eats every child except her own.

We have all been in situations such as that symbolized by the devouring mother: where there was only one explanation, only one truth, one way of feeling, of understanding. Some radical feminists are doing this — eating up every interpretation of history except one. And that is that all men are rotten and domineering and militaristic, and all women are earth mothers and naturally creation-centered.

That's the negative feminine at its worst, when it eats up all children except its own. Now, men can do that, too. The point is, we must be honest enough as we name the dark side of the masculine to also name the dark side of the feminine.

Negative femininity pulls us into unconsciousness. Into don't know, don't think, don't analyze, don't understand, don't explain — just stay home here with me and hold my hand. Enmeshment is somehow the substitute for strong love between individuals. If you were a good husband, you'd be home with me seven nights a week. And this, she thinks, is the perfect family — all sinking into great unconscious togetherness.

The situation is similar when the false feminine takes over the church. One can see it in certain retreat houses. It's like falling into the great whirlpool. It's "let's come to the retreat house and talk about our feelings." Nothing about social justice, nothing about the real world, nothing about the poor. Great religion begins in mysticism and always ends in politics. The false feminine creates priests preoccupied with temple religion and laymen whom we unkindly called "sanctuary rats." Domesticated into churchiness and liturgical paraphernalia. Read the seventh chapter of Jeremiah if you want to hear the prophetic man's response to the false feminine.

Finally, what happens in the womb has to be extracted from the womb. The penis is precisely that which opens the birth canal. Biology is destiny. The male knows this child can't stay in the womb; it has to get out and live. The male job is to lead us beyond the great unconscious into consciousness, clarity, decisiveness, the outer world of practical effect.

In the original Grail myth, when the Grail appears, usually right behind it is a woman holding a sword. The sword, at least in the earlier mythologies, is not a symbol of violence. It is a symbol of male discrimination: separating and understanding; refusing to get enmeshed in everything or get lost in false feeling or in the great unconscious and what we would today call sentimentality. This attribute is logos. The discriminating, clarifying word, an appropriate sense of boundaries.

Some feminist groups cannot tolerate this line of thinking. There is general encouragement for romantic expressionism, indulging of self-serving explanations and emotions that brook no contrary opinion or dialogue. Undisciplined bouts of feeling that build nothing positive but rather support victimhood and self-pity. (Even this explanation is anathema, and may not be spoken in politically correct circles!) It's gender affirmative action. They're saying, "All you males with your great ideas, what have you done to history? All you produced was war and greed and raping of the planet." And they're partly right.

But there is also a good side to the sword. There is a positive dimension to logos: reason, consciousness, understanding, discriminating. Without these, we are trapped in massive co-dependency. Too much subjectivity and mutual reinforcement of one another. (When women have discussed a gender issue together, there is a collusion that allows no contrary way of "feeling." It is as dogmatic and moralistic as any hierarchy ever was.)

You can unite only what is separate

When love does not understand separation, when it fails to see that if people are not first apart they cannot unite, that union can have no rich or healing meaning unless it comes from separateness — that's when you have co-dependency. I am so grateful someone created that word. Finally we have a term to describe the false meaning to an awful lot that is called love, to an awful lot that is called loyalty. Even in the church. Much of it is sick loyalty, negative co-dependency. It is not obedience to God, and it is not obedience to the great truth. Group strength can never be a substitute for lack of personal journey.

The masculine at its best knows how to make these discriminations, knows how to divide with the sword. We had a good example in the case of Solomon. Separate it — whatever it is — to find what's true over here and what's true over there. The very thing that men are so often criticized for — lack of feeling — is sometimes their unique gift. Detachment is necessary for sound discernment and healthy attachment.

Men should not give that up in the name of the great metaphorical feminine breasts. These make us feel warm and enmeshed, but we lose clarity. We lose our sense of the goal, all sense of meaning beyond enmeshment. It causes one to wonder how many of our marriages are co-dependent. Are these two people who have chosen to give themselves to one another, or two people who don't have a hint of who they are apart from one another? Perhaps keeping one another back from the journey? Identity and boundaries precede fruitful love relationships.

When Jesus calls his first men by the Sea of Galilee, the first two things he asks of them are acts of separation. They must separate from their jobs and their fathers (Matthew 4:18–22).

Family and job are the two things that keep us enmeshed. Most people cannot think beyond the family voices, beyond the way the family tells us how to get angry, for example. "We don't express anger in our family." No one said that directly, but we learned by the time we were four that it was the rule in our family. Or we are rageaholics. All we do is yell at one another. Pretty soon the yelling means nothing because everything occurs at the same volume.

Much that we call loyalty is merely fear. Fear of going on the journey. Fear of asking the real questions. Fear of being honest.

The church has exploited such fear-based loyalty. Many newly married and not-so-newly married couples have too. They call it loyalty, but all they have at the end is two bitter, defeated people. That cannot be the goal of grace. That cannot be the call of the Gospel, that the end product is two unhappy people who were "faithful" to one another for fifty years.

The same is true of the bitter, defeated people who, in the name of loyalty to the church, stayed in the ranks, but there's nothing there. I can out-orthodox anybody, but to my knowledge, orthodoxy has never healed anybody, never changed anybody, challenged anybody, inspired anybody, or helped anybody — because there is no power in it. That cannot be the great Gospel. It cannot be great truth. It is the false feminine. It is like children holding onto the skirts of Holy Momma Church.

When one breaks away from the great mother, the guilt and shame are phenomenal. The severing is at such a deep level that one can't feel good. If the things Momma first told us were not good, it's very difficult to change the emotional hardware.

Psychic incest

Something I did not expect to discover as much as I have in working with the men's movement is psychic incest. We have to name it. It's just as real as physical incest, and it is even harder to talk about. But, frequently, until we name it, most men do not even know that there is such a thing.

When we are "dear son," when we are Momma's boy, we do not want to lose that prize. It's heaven, it's utter security. Why leave Momma and bond with Daddy when Momma's bond is so wonderful?

Many men sell their souls for that. When men in later life talk deeply about their fathers, the affect is strikingly low. What we most commonly find are words like "sadness," "absence," and "I never knew him." They know they are supposed to love him, and want to, but it just did not happen, whatever "it" is. Father is this great mystery person. It is almost as if he does not have a face in some men's dreams. Usually the response is not anger, just sadness and absence and longing.

When, however, the same men talk about their mothers, the affect is high pitched. The words are of anger or love or confusion. There is tremendous guilt about even thinking anything negative about the greatest person in the world, about the ideal motherhood that goes with apple pie. But it is a very ambiguous relationship for many men.

There is the frequent feeling that "I was taken into my mother's favor, but I spent the rest of my life trying to get back out." For some men this results in a relationship that is love but is also experienced as rape. By contrast, I talked to some rapists at the jail where I am chaplain. Not one of them had a good relationship with his mother. So they go through life humiliating women to get back at the one who was supposed to tell them they were good but didn't. The rape problem is normally not lust; it's power, domination, humiliation.

At a less traumatic level, many men who experience this

same syndrome are merely incapacitated by it. We are not sure of our own feelings, do not know how to think apart from what Mom told us to think. That's why men need those exclusively male gatherings that have become so popular. Women have carried the feelings for men, have told us how to feel, and we are trying to re-learn a masculine mode of feeling that is not filtered through mother's approval, girl-friend's admiration, or wife's response. It is a totally new and liberating world for many men.

Most cultures have understood that the boy has to make a break from the incestuous feminine. Unless he is to some degree forced, he will not bond with the men. The great feminine is so sweet and so protective. The early experience and lifelong memory of that warmth can leave many men eternally searching for their mother. Many discover, years later, that they married their mother — especially if they married young or without much self-knowledge.

This is not necessarily a disaster, but it does lead at least to ambivalence. I love her but I can't stand her. I can't live with or without her. To some extent, of course, every man experiences that in relationship to the feminine. It is the ultimate fascination, the ultimate taboo, the ultimate every-thing. There is too much energy there. That's why the break has to happen. We had to break because we were submerged. Most men are somehow submerged in the eternal feminine.

Sinking into the feminine

The negative side of the feminine damages the man by con-fining him to the merely relational and subjective world, in the concrete, immediate, and momentary. "Just talk to me about now, forget your big ideas about the future." I recall how difficult it was when our New Jerusalem community started twenty years ago. The first household was thirteen young men and myself. Those guys — God, they had a vision: the Gospel, serving the world, helping the poor. We were going to change things.

We moved into a neighborhood and fixed up a house and we were only there three months when a whole group of girls moved in up the street. They were going to fix up a house and do the same thing we did. We were really grateful. The community looked whole. One household of men, one household of women. And then, of course, they started falling in love with one another. And that was good, too, for a while.

Then, suddenly, the guys were not talking about the kingdom anymore. They were not talking about helping the poor anymore. When I came back to the community after a visit to the Third World, and started talking about social justice, it was the young men who fought me. They had found the sweetest, most wonderful community, with all this feminine love and nurture, pot lucks, sitting around sharing their feelings in the evenings and playing the guitar and having three-hour Masses at which everybody was crying. The men just sank into it. They wanted to stay in that state of bliss forever. They did not want to *do* anything.

Instead, it was the girls who, when I came back from the Third World, were ready to go off to Nicaragua. "Let's go and do it." The men had just discovered the feminine and wanted to stay there for good. The women, by contrast, were discovering their masculine side and ready to "do it."

Many of the most heroic things have been done by women. In the Catholic Church, the clergy are at least twenty years behind the nuns. And behind the rest of the church, too. Some of the seminarians to whom I preach retreats are all engrossed in decorating the sanctuary. Liturgy is everything. The whole deal is to get the people to come. Where I happen to be king and on the throne and in charge. It's easy to recognize the men lost in the feminine. They are into dressing up. Their whole deacon year is spent picking out their vestments and vessels. I call it the "church of Leviticus" as opposed to the courageous "church of Exodus." Ecclesiastical, in-house concerns instead of making outer connections with the streets, the society, the larger family.

When I was ordained in 1970, I arrogantly thought that all priests who came after me would think like *me!* But, sadly, I can't even talk to these guys. They walk out on me. When I started giving priests' retreats — the first one was seventeen years ago — the old priests would walk out. Now it is the newly ordained who walk out.

If they are forced by the bishop to come, they sit in the back row wearing the full Roman collar (there's a new kind out, twice as wide as the old one). I don't know whom they are trying to convince.

In fairness it should be noted that they grew up in a chaotic world. They did not have a sense of boundaries, or identity, such as I was given in the 1940s and 1950s. I had time to build my tower. I had Sister Ephraim. Then, when the 1960s came, I could jump off the tower. But these guys who grew up in the 1960s and 1970s and the silliness of the 1980s don't have a sense of boundaries, identity, or tradition.

We're seeing this trend across the board, not just in the Catholic Church. Fundamentalism, neoconservatism is a phenomenon all over the earth. There are more than five billion of us on the planet now, scrambling for the limited resources and not sure we're going to make it. So we are all looking for our own tiny identity. Some call it the Yugoslavia syndrome, as we reject the scary bigger world for the smaller security systems.

Without true kings and warriors we're not going to make it. We'll just sink into the soft lover and the cheap magician. That's what we did in the 1970s. No John the Baptist came to remind us about "out there." The world is bigger than America, bigger than the Catholic Church. No one should try to make the king of kings into a tribal god, or make the Lord of the Universe into our little self-serving monarch who holds together our tiny world.

Today, the ideal is to be mutual and egalitarian, with a determination not to let anybody be leader. That way, no one can have control over our lives. That way, *we* can finally be in control. There is a terrible distrust of the possibility of the good king. To ensure nothing happens, we limit everything to process.

Liberals cannot be dogmatic about content — that would not be liberal. So they get dogmatic about process. At a meeting in California, they had gathered several groups together and I was supposed to address them. We had only one day to deal with some rather heavy stuff. But we spent three quarters of the day discussing the logistics of the day. Some women in the group did not want me to be seen as leader. They could not say that, so they figured they'd bury the day in process.

First, they insisted that I not be standing while I addressed them, because then it would look as if I were better than they. So, could we have a table? Then, could we have a woman sit at the table, and we should sit equidistant from the center of the table, I on one side and the woman on the other. And *she* would monitor the meeting. She would tell me when I could talk. Fine by me. Less work.

People just started leaving the room. Yet, the process people would not give up. Then, the table solution was not satisfactory. In all this they never attacked me. They concentrated on the process. We lost half the group in one day — people who had given up work days to be there. "Process-control" ate up all children except their own, and then there was none. Political correctness was itself their only child.

The dominant attitude was: There's only one way in which to reorganize the world. That way entails that men never have power, that men are never allowed to speak without controls and limits, that men are shown they are not the leaders and cannot be trusted.

Healthy masculinity is not the same thing as patriarchy, but patriarchy and dominative power have abused so many on this earth that it will take us a long time to heal and trust men again.

Whose side are you on?

We can't build with that kind of overreaction. Yet it is likely to last for a while. It needs to be named and described, not to make anyone angry but so that men will be aware of it and won't be surprised by it. I don't think it will build a new creation. It's too petty. It's too small, too angry, too fear-filled. It's not yet Gospel. The Gospel always stands in the middle and holds the breach together at the cost of the self. Look at the cross just as a geometric symbol. Christ is killed on the intersection of opposites and pays the price in *his own* body — not in other people's.

Whenever people try to hold things together, to build a bridge, they suffer. Some men thought I was a wimp for cooperating with the process that day in California. By even daring to come that day and present myself as a speaker, those women thought I was a patriarchal pig. So I couldn't win. I could have just left, I suppose. Why bother with such stuff?

The way to bother with it, in my opinion, is to stand in between and speak truth on both sides. But when you speak truth on both sides, normally neither side will hear you or fully accept you. For me, the insight of the Gospel is this: We must build the bridge. We must be the *pontifex*, the bridge builder. We cannot build a bridge from the middle. We have to build a bridge from one side. The Gospel says you must build a bridge from the side of the disempowered ones. (This is divine revelation. Common sense or culture have never reached this conclusion; only God reveals it.)

Start on the side of the poor. Start on the side of the losers, the victims, the powerless. In that sense we must stand on the side of our sisters who have been oppressed by this patriarchal culture.

We need the courage to recognize, however, that on a lot of levels men also are oppressed, men also are hurting and feeling disempowered and castrated, rejected and misunderstood. That, too, is a place of powerlessness from which to build a bridge.

When I addressed the male chapter of another religious order, to which the female provincials had also been invited, one of the women at this men's chapter raised her hand and snapped, "I don't like you talking about masculine spirituality. You've had masculine spirituality throughout all history." I replied that it has not been masculine spirituality, it has been neuter spirituality. Now we are ready for a "holy marriage" between mature men and mature women — true partnership.

I am not advocating patriarchy. I am talking about rediscovering the truth that is on both sides. But first we men have to discover what is healthy about a masculine spirituality. That nun did not accept my response, I don't think. But more to the point was the atmosphere in the room. "You're not going to disagree with the nuns," the tension in the room seemed to be saying. You disagree with them and you're dead.

So I tried to steer the middle course. But one can't. That's how polarized we are today. That's how great the mistrust is.

I'm using church examples, but married people know this is also applicable in the marriage relationship. A massive fear, one of the other. Someone must stand in the breach, build the bridges, and start on the side of those who are weaker. That is the Gospel way.

At least know the question

The word "quest" comes from the same root as the word "question." We cannot go on a quest until we know what the question is. And the male journey is fundamentally a clarifying of the question. God is the answer, but in between is the clarifying. That is where the discriminating sword comes in, hacking away to get to the real name and shape of the self.

At first, Parsifal thinks the object of his quest is to meet the wonderful, secure, eternal, feminine out there that will take care of him. As he progresses on the journey, however, the question is clarified. And that is what keeps him going on the quest.

Whom does the Grail serve? That is the question to which we are slowly learning the answer. What am I doing this for? Why am I feeling this feeling? This anger? This pain? And unless we feel it, unless we go down into the grief, into the depths, into the great unconscious, pulled into the labyrinth, normally we won't know the deeper answers. We will have stayed on the level of life's superficial questions, which is precisely not to go on the quest.

Chapter 4

Energy for the quest _____

The descent stage of the quest for the Holy Grail is where the terror begins. And the miracles. These extraordinary phenomena provoke us to ask what kind of people wrote such stories as the Grail myth. What kind of world did they experience? What were they expecting? The stories lead us to suspect they already had at least some kind of momentary Grail experience.

There is in all of us some memory of primal union that refuses to go away. It is tied up with our mothers, and through them with the eternal feminine. It can be partially understood and renewed through each friendship or each loving, mirrors of that primal union.

The feeling is one of once being twinned. We are now divided from whatever or whoever we were twinned with, and we're forever looking for the missing part. The result is a radical sense of being unwhole. Thus we are restless all our lives.

Search for our other half

We are still strangers to ourselves and can't seem to find ourselves except through a search for the other. The original union experience creates this yearning for the twin, for the beloved, for the "not me." This becomes the yearning for God, the final other.

I personally find this alienation and subsequent yearning less overwhelming than when I was young, perhaps because I have partially found something of what I sought. But the longing for the beloved is still there, and in some ways deeper. I'm looking for my soul double, my partner, my other half, to whom I belong and from whom my soul emerges.

I also sometimes experience that someone is longing for me, maybe more than I for that someone. We who are lucky enough to have this experience often wonder who is calling us, whom we are trying to remember. What is the face I'm looking for and waiting for? What is it that reminds me of her or him? What looks like him or her?

Maybe this question — this quest — is the only one that needs to be pursued. I think some kind of identification with the beloved is the necessary energy for the spiritual quest. That is what healthy Christianity has done. It has given the soul this image of the beloved, an image that told us God was okay. It is called Jesus.

That quest was harder for the male, because the other half appeared like another male, Jesus Christ. The natural mirror image, at least to the heterosexual male soul, is feminine. The man is looking for that to be imaged in a feminine way. What we experience when we identify with the beloved — this is the achievement of the saints and mystics — is not "I love you by choice or devotion" but "I am you." That's the identification that happens on the spiritual journey. As Jesus put it, "I and the Father are one."

The object of devotion is not even out there anymore; it has been so taken in that I am over there and the "over there" is in here. One way this is symbolized is communion.

That's what propels the quest forward — the experience of being twinned and yet divided. We must hold on to both. We're always searching for the other half and finding it symbolized here and there and falling in love with it; we're always falling in love with what we are not yet. Wherever it is imaged, there is a part of our souls. We go around grabbing: there! there! I want this and I want that, I want her, I want him, this will give me the other part of my soul.

But it is never "it." We continue the quest. To this end, it is somehow easier to identify with the *image* of the beloved than with the image of God. That is why, in Christianity, Jesus was called the mediator, the one in between.

It doesn't help, either, that the best things can't be talked about. No one has seen God. How does one fall in love with God? When people say, "I love God," we're glad they say so and that they want to love God, and we know they mean it, but then, who is God? All we have are the metaphors, the images, the beloveds who keep showing us their faces. We say, "Ah, that's it," and we go after it. We fall in love with it. We draw close, and we are almost always disappointed.

So we live in a kind of ongoing radical dissatisfaction. That is the essentially tragic nature of human life. That is why life is hard — I don't know any other way to say it. If we're authentically living it, if we're on the quest, life is lonely. We don't want to live that loneliness. We find it easier to live with a kind of idolatry — creating something, anything, that will fill up the hole — or to keep ourselves artificially stimulated, which will make us think we're satisfied.

Driven forward, pulled back, that's us

Parsifal's mother, in some versions of the Grail story, is named "Heart Sorrow." Her goodness to him, her neediness for him, keep him forever trapped in this yearning, in this guilt, in this grief. We will see it throughout the whole quest. It sends him forward, yet it pulls him back.

That's the dilemma of the feminine. It's the energy for the quest, but it's also what pulls us back. That's why male-female relationships are so difficult. We never know which one is at work when, the moving forward or being drawn back. Do we succumb to it and get lost in the whirlpool, or do we listen to it with sensitivity and find it's also the very yearning and longing that propels us forward?

Heart Sorrow, when she sees he is going to leave her, gives

Parsifal three commands. Momma's rules. First, respect all women. That's a very good rule and we find it in all the codes of the knights. It means: Respect the feminine, respect the soul, the sensitive, the intuitive, the erotic, the earthy. Respect Mother Earth.

One of the reasons women are so angry at us men is because they're tired of being devalued. Western civilization is tired of the feminine being devalued. It's tired of the rational, the command-and-control model, the negative masculine running everything.

So Heart Sorrow's first rule is: Always respect women. That's the positive side. But, she adds, get the ring from the woman. That's going to be the hero's first mistake, listening to Momma on this one. The first woman he meets he wants to get engaged to, get the ring — or give the ring. Momma is saying, tie her down, make her a wife.

The mother's second rule was: "Go to church every day, and there you'll get all the food you need." What mother hasn't told her sons and daughters that? Go to church. And it's true: If we really gain access to the symbols, we'll get all the food we need. It is mother love that drives most men toward religion, compassion, and the search for God.

The third rule is interesting: "Don't ask any questions." The mother's third rule becomes the central problem for Parsifal. What will inhibit the hero from keeping his goal is that he didn't ask the question. And the reason is: His mother told him not to! When you ask questions, people won't like you. And Mother always wants her son to be popular. But what she is also saying implicitly is: Don't be aware, remain in the great unconscious sea. Don't use the discriminating sword to move into consciousness and awareness and answers and wisdom. Remain, instead, in the great collective. Think like everyone else thinks.

That's the false feminine, pulling the masculine into passivity and unawareness. Don't say critical things about the church, it warns. Don't be critical of the political party. Accept it all and people will like you.

It's a very easy seduction because on a certain level it works. You don't stand for much, but you're a nice guy, it soothes. You can hang out at the bar and you won't create any problems. You can be a member of the parish council, even though you don't really stand for the Gospel. Just be a nice member. Go along with everything.

Many clergy and other shapers of our culture often do little more than repeat this litany: Respect women and get engaged quickly; go to church and get all the food you want; don't ask questions and people will like you.

Those three rules are both wisdom and stupidity. After all, we got them from our mothers, where our soul quest began. But beware: The mother's goodness and neediness keep the hero in grief and guilt and yearning to "return to the womb." He is compelled to keep running back to Momma.

He's halfway down the road and he runs back because he feels guilty he hasn't called home for several months. That's emotional incest. The guilt that comes from knowing Momma is displeased is almost bottomless. Mother can be eighty-eight years old and we can be sixty, and one little word from her slays the hero with self-doubt.

Dante bitten by the archetype

Dante's image of the feminine is classic and will help us understand the Grail quest. He got this feminine image from a woman he saw when he was nine years old. Her name was Beatrice. When he finally reaches the height of the *Paradiso*, after exploring the *Purgatorio* and *Inferno*, even at that point Dante never looks directly at God. He looks at Beatrice and Beatrice looks at God. Right at the end of his quest, he knows God on *her* face. He just keeps looking at her and knows God. In that final scene, the sun and moon and stars and love are all one. He has achieved his life's perfection, completed the journey he began as a nine-year-old boy.

Of that boyhood experience Dante wrote that "the spirit

of life, which has its dwelling in the secret chambers of the heart, began to tremble so violently that my body shook and in trembling said these words, 'Behold, a deity stronger than I is coming to rule me.' "

That is possession. When archetypes grab the soul, they are imperialistic. We are ruled by them. From that time forward, Dante wrote, "love quite governed my soul."

That becomes the story of the rest of his life. When he is eighteen, he sees her again on the streets of Florence. "This same wonderful lady appeared to me, dressed this time in pure white.... She's really an angel coming out of the heavens. And, passing through the street, she turned her eyes where I stood, sorely abashed. And by her unspeakable courtesy she saluted me with so virtuous a bearing that I seemed then and there to behold the limits of blessedness."

Who wouldn't give his life for that? And the heterosexual male ought to acknowledge that the homosexual male has a similar experience with another man. We had better start understanding that. Homosexuals have their own journey to walk, and they too have to find through that image of the beloved the eternal image of God. Same-sex love is not going to go away because Western civilization doesn't like it or is unwilling to deal with it.

Homosexuality is a surprise that God throws into nature. Just when we think we've got perfect order, God always creates some disorder. Just to upset us, I'm convinced. Reality is always order mixed with disorder. I don't mean disorder in the sense that a recent Vatican document used it. I mean, it breaks the pattern just when we thought we had the pattern figured out. God alone is in charge and in control.

The Navajo rug, if it's a spiritual rug, has to have a spirit line woven in it, and this spirit line is an imperfection. The spirit gets into the rug not through the perfect part but through the imperfect part. In some Native American cultures, the homosexual person was the shaman, the medicine man, because he combined the masculine and feminine in one person. The rest of us also are bisexual, in the sense of having the capacity to love both sexes. And we all want, to a greater or lesser degree, to combine the masculine and feminine.

Some cultures look on this as a healthy advancement and others look on it as unhealthy. Those cultures that look on it as unhealthy, in my opinion, have an excessive need for order. The Anglo-Saxon and Northern European cultures, for example, resent disorder, anything that breaks the pattern. What we want when we look for order is, basically, control. The ego likes control.

That's why Jesus tells us not to judge. Judgments are ways of looking for control, for fitting people and events into consistent formulas, even when the formulas do not match reality. This is the attitude of the false king, wanting a pseudo-sense of being empowered. The true king can pull everything within the circle, even the imperfect, even the flaw in the rug, even the so-called disordered.

Man is stuck with a feminine side

The conscious part of maleness is the sword, discernment, logic, clarity, explanation, the word. When our Protestant brothers and sisters put the pulpit in the middle of the altar, they were enthroning the masculine. They have little left but the word, and that's too masculine. There is little room for Mary or the eternal feminine. No room for the soul, really, because the soul cannot be grasped by the verbal.

When the conscious self is masculine, the feeling world moves into the unconscious. The soul, the erotic world, the body world — that's where we men are most awkward. We'd much sooner talk in the world of ideas. Put a group of men together, and everything is reduced to opinions. Religion and politics — a whole night in the bar and it's all opinions. It's hard to create community with only men. Five hundred men, five hundred opinions.

Usually we let women carry the feeling world; we don't

know how to do it. The women do the feeling for the family, for the marriage. In the relationship and feeling world the woman moves with self-confidence. She in turn is at her weakest when she moves into the world of opinions and what males call objectivity.

Men are at their weakest when they are pulled unwittingly into the inner world of the feminine. We call this an "anima attack."

The anima takes over in proportion to men's failure to recognize and respect feminine values in themselves, in life, and in women. The man will then feel a dark mood, and he won't know where it came from. The moodiness grabs like a demon and he wants to say something cruel, to be petty and peevish. He will hate himself, hate everything. It's ugly, the male at his worst. One word from a woman can get him into it. One look — the Medusa look — can do it. Or absence of contact with a woman. He becomes sulky, overly sensitive, waiting for someone to do something so he can get mad. It's as though he is immersed in a psychological fog. A wimp in a whirlpool of subjectivity.

The giveaway is that he wants to withdraw from relationship. (For the wrong reasons; there's also a good time to go into solitude.) But now his relationship skills are not functioning, so he has to hide. That's why men have things like dens where they can go and shut the door. Or he hides behind the newspaper or in front of the television set.

If a man argues or writes, for example, when in the grip of such an attack, the anima influence can be seen in sarcasm, innuendos, and irrelevancies that reveal a subjective bias and detract from reality. When he is trying to hurt the other guy, he's having an anima attack.

On the other hand, when he can be fair and keep his gloves on, he's in a healthy masculine mode.

When a man inflicts the anima attack on his wife, going for the jugular, trying to shame or hurt, he's making a double fool of himself. She can play that game better than her husband any day. He will always lose. The man simply does not have the skills. That's the woman's conscious world while it's his unconscious world, and he will be awkward and off balance.

To cope, we have to dig down into our unconscious. The military and business worlds teach people to put the lid on, as macho fathers teach their sons to put the lid on, and the result is that such sons have no access to the anima, their feminine soul.

Because a man has no skills to go down there, what usually happens is that he hands that whole world over to the woman. He goes away to earn money and stays away from home as much as possible and goes to the bar afterward where he can talk to other men. They won't pull him into this whirlpool where he is not at home, which he does not comprehend.

If he had a wise mother who let him have his feelings and own his feelings, he would have had a head start. But if his mother disallowed the feeling world, and told him what to feel, how to be masculine, then he has a lot of work to do. He doesn't practice the male mode of feeling because he never had any practice. Women always did it for him. It takes so long, many of us will never totally work it through.

And, of course, none of us had a perfect mother, so we all have some wounds in this area. Every mom was busy at times and told us to shut up. We eventually learned that things went better if we hid our feelings or, better, didn't have any. It was the male way to survive. Yet, if a man does not find some way to express his feelings, the anima attack will only get worse. We must learn skills to get what's inside out, ritualize it, because it's not going to be driven away by our refusal to bring it to consciousness. If we leave it in the unconscious, we will simply get into deeper and deeper anima attacks.

We all know older men who have been submerged in the negative feminine for decades. They stop feeling, stop talking. They are the grandfathers who just sit in the corner at family gatherings and don't say anything. That's the price we pay for years of refusing to feel. Pretty soon, we don't know how.

Psychologist Carl Jung wrote: "The anima intensifies, exaggerates, and falsifies all emotional relationships that a man has with his work and with all other people of both sexes. The antidote for this is for the man to know what he is feeling and become capable of expressing this in some kind of relatedness." Maybe you have to go off long enough to get clarity. But don't stay away too long. Finally you have to bring the feeling back into relationship where it is meant to be expressed.

One technique of Marriage Encounter is teaching people how to argue. They teach people literally to hold hands and make eye contact, and as long as they can do this they can say whatever they want. They can say, "Honey, I'm with you, but when you do that you make me damn mad." Both parties, of course, get to say their piece, but the male finds it harder. Masculine spirituality is an art of separation. We're always separating and going out. But that's our dark side. We want to separate too quickly and not talk it out, but hurts only fester in unhealthy solitude and separation.

Beware the woman's animus

The *animus* is the masculine part of a woman. It shows her in her worst state, when she gets opinionated. It has nothing to do with logic as men define that. It has nothing to do with what we think makes sense and frequently seems to have nothing to do with the issues you were talking about. When a woman is in an animus attack, she is trapped in her own unconscious, and irrational feelings are going to pour out.

I remember my dad trying to argue with my mother, and I always took the side of my father. I could see my mother, who is an Eight on the enneagram, just take off into what seemed to my male mind completely illogical. I'd say to myself, that has nothing to do with the point, but to her it was the only point. I finally understood when I discovered it was an animus attack.

Psychologist John Sanford wrote in *The Invisible Partners:* "The animus is master of opinions in a woman. It expresses itself in judgments, massive generalizations, critical statements, and apodictic assertions that do not come from a woman's own process of thinking and feeling, but have been picked up from various authoritative sources: mother, father, books, articles." They're looking for the authority they feel they don't have.

Men do the same thing in an anima attack — they get petty about external authorities. Because they're not that sure of themselves. Whenever someone is opinionated, it probably means he is not that sure of himself. True authority is authoritative, but never gets this "pettiness of opinionatedness," if I may put it that way.

Fundamentally, we tend to be confused in an anima attack. This often leads us to be negative as a way to defend ourselves. We're in the whirlpool. We do not understand. So we try to find our old ground by getting apodictic and adamant and falsely negative and falsely masculine. We bring out our sword too quickly, before we have reached discernment. We lose our creativity, we lose our imagination.

A woman in an animus attack is similarly not creative. She does not draw on her life-giving, imaginal sources of resolution or healing. Instead, the opinions of the animus have a peculiarly irritating effect on other people, because in spite of their seeming logic they don't really fit the situation. They can't be reasoned with because the animus has an absolutist attitude and the opinions are not amenable to discussion or qualification. Whenever the animus takes over a woman, she is taken away from her own thinking and sinks to banal statements, sweeping judgments, and generalizations. I call it the witch ascending on her broom. (Her feast day is October 31. We must always symbolize the unconscious.)

That's when we have to be sympathetic. At that point she's often hating herself. The attack looks like it's directed at the other, but she's feeling very insecure herself. And that's why often she will break into tears halfway through. She knows she's losing it. But she's feeling something.

What can we do at that point? We should not get out our sword and try to explain anything to her. We should hold her. We must move to the symbolic, the creative, and imaginative. It is not solved in the head. It is not a matter of logos. If you move in and try to explain her to herself, you'll probably get another attack. It would be futile to explain a woman from a man's perspective because you probably are not understanding it anyway.

Boy sets sights on men's world

Back to Parsifal. He insists on leaving home, on leaving the mother, setting out on the journey. The only woman he has lived with is his mother, so it was from her he received the essential preparation for his journey.

His first encounter is with the five knights — a massive show of male energy. The five knights are in full armor, and his first reaction is to wonder whether they are gods or angels.

That's the little boy looking at Star Wars. It's the boy watching Mr. Universe or the Olympic Games. It's just awesome male power, male speed, male height. It is everything a boy, whether he is eight or eighteen, wants to be. It is his other half, and he's willing to leave mother, sweet mother, because he has to find the five knights. He is fascinated by the coach, the teacher, the idol — almost anybody but his father.

Fathers, of whatever culture, are not the initiators of their sons. Boys have always been initiated by an uncle or an unrelated male — by someone other than the father — because the energy is too strong between the son and his father. There is too much confusion, too much hurt, too much expectation, too much need, too much desire.

The father was the boy's first god-figure, along with the

mother. Humans need the image of the divine. They can't go straight to it. It can't even adequately be talked about. So we need to look at God through a lover or a beloved, who becomes an image of the divine.

Some of our disappointment in our fathers is because we expected too much from them, and no other person was assigned to be the initiator. The Navajos always have an uncle do it. He teaches the young one about sexuality and spirituality — and about pain. Pain is part of the spirituality. Dad can't "teach" that, although he can *model* forbearance and long-suffering.

Yet, Parsifal is looking for his father, for his own maleness, for the mentor, for men to guide and teach him. What he asks for is their armor. And one of them gives it to him. And what he then does is masterful mythology: He puts the armor on over his mother's homespun clothes. He does not take his mother's clothes off and put the armor on; the story is specific that he kept his mother's clothes on. He's flirting with the masculine without letting go of Momma's homespun wisdom.

He is also fascinated by the knights' horses. He wants a horse, he wants armor, all the symbols of masculine power. And once he has these, he is possessed by the male archetype. He sets off on his horse, with his armor over his homespun garments, and for the moment at least he forgets the feminine world. He forgets Momma for the first time in his life. The only time he will go back to her is when he longs to see her, when he longs to know she still loves him, or when he needs food or new clothes. He's still convinced his mother has to pick out his clothes.

So he travels on his horse, with his armor, down the road. The first place he comes to is the Devastated Convent and Monastery. On the monastery grounds the crops won't grow, the animals won't reproduce, the well of the monastery church is dried up. They have built the temple over the well, but the well underneath is dry. Doesn't that say it all!

The drying up of the church

Interestingly enough, the oldest versions say the sacrament is there. But the monks and nuns can't approach it or use it. We're in mythic language. God's presence is there but we do not have access to it anymore. This is the wasteland image. Not only is the whole kingdom a wasteland under the Fisher King, but the church itself is a wasteland. And the monks and nuns have no access to the sacrament.

God has not abandoned the church. Christ is still in it, but we don't know how to recognize Christ.

We're still early in the story, so, as yet, Parsifal has no strength to do anything about all this. He just looks at it, and promises that one day he will return and do something about it. He has not discovered Spirit yet, does not know what to do, because he himself has not walked the journey.

This is the first apparition of what's broken about things. The church isn't working; things are in a state of spiritual emergency. Among other things this reminds us that the spiritual emergency did not first happen in the 1990s; there is always a spiritual emergency.

He leaves. He meets a nameless woman in a tent. Because he has never left home before, he thinks all big buildings are churches. When he sees this big tent and thinks it is a church and sees a woman inside, he follows his mother's instructions, approaches the woman, and eats at her table. He takes the ring from her finger and puts it on his finger, right after the meal.

(This is an appropriate occasion to note again that there's not just one interpretation of these stories, so each of us is free to make our own. Thus, my version here is only one among many possibilities.)

The woman immediately asks him to leave because she is already engaged. And so he does. One interpretation is that she's nameless to Parsifal because he is still unaware of the feminine, he is still under the influence of his mother. So he has not truly met this woman as an individual. This is rather like a boy's first sexual experience. She is not "Gail" or "Theresa." She's just a woman, she has breasts, she is the feminine, and that alone turns him on.

Likewise the reason he thinks the tent is a church is because he has not grown up yet, and this is his first venture into religion. Similarly, our first baptism, our first Jesus experience, is not the real thing yet. This is another reason Parsifal leaves rather quickly — it's not the real thing. It's a minor Grail experience, perhaps a goad or invitation, and it's a start, but not the real thing. And the woman is just a conquest, as today's young man might say. He eats at her table, puts her ring on his finger, and moves on, hopefully wiser.

Then he meets the Red Knight. In the English version, the story has become King Arthur and the Knights of the Round Table. In the Round Table story, the king has created a realm of perfect union where all are brothers. Roundness always symbolizes completeness and totality. You never have totality in a circle unless there is a king, unless someone has kingly energy holding it together. It does not have to be *just* one person, but there must be *at least* one person who has king or queen energy. Otherwise the siblings will fight and fracture any possible wholeness.

All the knights are sent out from the Round Table. Their point of departure is this wholeness. And they all return there. A warrior is always dangerous if he is not in submission to a king. When the warrior loses contact with the wisdom of the king to tell him which battles are worth fighting and which are not, he is in trouble. So the Red Knight has been sent forth from Arthur's Round Table. And the king sent word that Parsifal can have the armor of the Red Knight — if he can get it.

Red is common symbolism for the male. It's blood, it's passion, it's fury, it's fire, it's excitement — in many mythologies the male color. When the Red Knight appears on the road — again, like an apparition — he's dressed in red, and he holds a gold cup. There it is again, the invitation to the Grail. We see it along the way momentarily. It's the promise.

Boy flirts with manhood

Parsifal immediately kills the Red Knight with his sword, piercing him through the eye. It seems the first need of the young man is to compete: to win against other masculine energy, to convince himself that he has it. Look at little ten-year-old boys. They're just full of male energy, fighting and hitting against each other; you can't stop it; they go on all day, competing: Mine is bigger than yours; my dad is bigger than yours; I'm better, bigger, whatever. They're looking for their Red Knight. Looking for their own power.

Thank God for sports. In a certain sense, thank God for military training. One wishes they wouldn't fight wars, but I don't know what other controlled outlet there would be for this energy. Boys seem to need to march around camps and hold guns on their shoulders, pretending they're strong. Somewhere this urge has to be ritualized. Now that we don't understand the spiritual warrior anymore, that's all we have left.

This need to build the tower is not going to go away. It's innate in the male to want to be stronger, to win and compete. Look at the young warriors in the business world; look at the political world; it's the same game, the same energy. It's the necessary "heroic instinct" needed to grow men beyond selfishness. But if it is not guided, it actually preserves men in selfishness!

Young Parsifal should indeed be fighting in this game, sixty-year-old men in the Senate should be kings, not warriors, should not be needing to show their swords and their power and trying to prove that "mine is bigger than yours."

Now, Parsifal again takes the Red Knight's armor and puts it over his homespun clothes. It is a mask, a mere persona he is trying on. Now I am my father, I am a man, I am the Red

Knight. Aggression and heroics are necessary in the early period. He rides the horse of the Red Knight all day and all night because he does not know how to stop it. He learned how to get on it, but he can't stop it. Similarly, he doesn't know how to take off his armor. That's the teenage boy. He doesn't know when to quit. There are no kings around telling him to let go. It was fun to play baseball for an hour, but now he needs to learn how to be a human being again.

He ignores the golden cup that the Red Knight came carrying; he doesn't take it on his journey. It is the promise of redeemed masculinity. It's a hint but he misses it. And he does not go back to King Arthur, so he does not enter into wholeness around the Round Table. Arthur has to send for him.

I have learned gradually that it isn't always the father rejecting the son. Many sons spend their twenties and thirties rejecting their father. "He rejected me, I'm going to reject him back." "He hurt me, I'm gonna get him back." Parsifal will not go to Arthur. Arthur keeps sending word out — send Parsifal to me, I want to reward him.

But Parsifal never goes back to the Round Table, never returns to Arthur's castle. So Arthur has to search for him, and even vows to find him. This is the father yearning for his son, for the completeness of having the son, hankering for the maturity of the warrior, learning to bring the warrior under the aegis of the king and thus bring it all together. It is also Jesus' story of the Prodigal Son.

Soon afterward, Parsifal, though still unable to put a stop to his adventures, begins again to miss his mother. He feels guilty about leaving her. He turns back to find her. On the way, he comes upon a castle.

What's leading him back? Is it an anima attack or is it the Grail? Always, it's both. Half good and half bad. But he's still on the quest. He is starting to learn the questions. And he turns back. In turning back to find Momma, he finds this other castle.

Chapter 5

The Grail experience _____

Zen masters traditionally did not allow a young man to come and study spirituality until he was at least thirty-five. Carl Jung imposed similar restrictions at his institute in Zurich. And in the Roman Catholic Church there have been comparable guidelines in Canon Law, for example, that one could not become a bishop before thirty-five.

We are not given the age of Parsifal, but we assume that at the time of our story he was already grown up. When a man sets out on the journey too quickly, he is not likely to know what the questions are, especially if he does not have a father or mentor to guide him.

Thus, if he has a Grail experience, he is likely to use it for his own ego inflation. If it attaches him to the holy too quickly, he does not know what to do with it except say, "Ain't I special." To have a Grail experience before he has suffered is, frankly, dangerous. He still builds his tower, but it is a spiritual (ideologically correct) tower, and therefore impregnable, sometimes even by God.

You have to start slowly

That's why, when the Grail enters a young man's life, it appears veiled. This became a very relevant issue for me in the early years of our New Jerusalem community in Ohio, composed, basically, of myself and a thousand teenagers. There, I saw the danger of religious experience that is protected,

97

hovered over, and talked about, where you have a bunch of eighteen-year-old boys all gung-ho to be holy and right. It doesn't, of itself, lead to true wisdom.

This myth should make more sense for folks somewhere in the middle of life. Younger men should recall that Jesus did not have a full Grail experience until he was thirty. Then he went into the wilderness. Observe how he understands the suffering, goes into the darkness, understimulates himself. He leaves the world of productivity and efficiency and success. Then, in the midst of meaninglessness, he hears, "You are my beloved son." Only that changes his life. We had not heard anything about him for thirty years except that he was born, that he was circumcised, and at twelve rebelled against his mother (Luke 2:41–52).

That's a Grail experience of a minor kind, when a boy leaves Momma and seeks "the house of his father." We must leave home, the domestic world of Mom, to find our larger male home. The church always had a hard time preaching about that: How could Jesus treat the Blessed Virgin Mary this way? But even Jesus had to break out and "be about his Father's business" (Luke 2:49). If a man does not break from the too easy comfort of Mom, he simply doesn't become a man. Unfortunately, some of us simply traded Mom for a coddling wife or for the clergy perks of Holy Momma Church!

Hey, Parsifal, this here's your godfather

Let us return to the great myth of the Holy Grail. Parsifal starts to feel guilty for not having called home all this time. He turns back to find his mother. On the way he finds this castle.

In the castle, he meets the one we would call his godfather. Gournamond is the name given him in some versions of the legend. We get the impression Parsifal lives with him for some time. This is the castle of masculinity, the castle where the godfather, the goodfather, teaches the boy. It is a symbol of initiation. Very often, especially if the son had an abusive father who either physically or verbally abused him or emotionally demeaned him in any way, there is a desperate need in the boy for a godfather.

The godfather tradition did not develop by accident but because it was needed. This is where the boy could go for refuge. A good example was the case of St. Francis, who was at the receiving end of a very abusive relationship with his father. So, whenever he returned to Assisi from where he lived outside the walls, he would be in fear of running into his old man. We're told his father would begin to curse him and say what an embarrassment Francis was to him. Assisi was then, and indeed still is, a very small town. One can picture Francis coming through the gate and seeing his father coming down the road.

It hurts so much to have his father curse him, to have him say he's an embarrassment to the family business, that Francis brings in a beggar. He tells this beggar: "When my dad starts calling me all these terrible names, come up and whisper in my other ear that I'm good, a son of God, that I'm beloved." Or some such words. That's the godfather. Marvelous psychodrama! We all need a good father in some ways, but none more than the son who has an abusive father.

The father-son relationship more often becomes abusive in the case of the oldest son, especially if the son is more talented or on a different track than the father, if his life appears a rejection of the father's lifestyle. And most of all if he's the mother's favorite.

Most of the men I have worked with in jails and youth ministry who were physically abused by their dads were beloved of their mother. The dynamic is easy to figure out.

This married man has been receiving all the love of this woman. Then, when the woman has her first child, especially if it is a boy, she transfers her love overnight. The husband feels the rejection and is hurt, to say the least. The son feels it and naturally loves it — all the attention and affection from his mother. But eventually he realizes his dad doesn't like him. The dad, in turn, feels a kind of guilt. He gets these confused feelings — remember the confused feeling world of the male — "Why don't I like my own flesh and blood?"

It is classic jealousy: They are both in love with the same woman. And, of course, the same woman is in love with both of them. But she is putting most of her nourishing love into her son, and it can lead to a very frightening relationship between the father and son. The little boy grows up doing everything he can to please his father. "What can I do to get this guy to like me?" No matter what he tries, it doesn't work, and he gets beaten down.

The dark king is at work here. He cannot love others unless they worship him. He wants his sons to worship him. When the son, on the other hand, has been made so self-assured by the mother that in a sense he doesn't need the father, naturally the father feels rejected. The son does not admire, honor, or even want the father.

It never enters the son's mind that he is in some ways rejecting his father. This is because the son is so secure in his mother's love. The dad will already say to him when he's four or five: Do you want to go out and do this or that? And the son replies: No, I'd sooner stay here. He wants to stay home and be with Mom. He does not know he is rejecting the dad, but the dad feels a rejection. Even little David can kill Goliath.

Parsifal comes to the castle of the good father, the one who is going to take care of him, the "male mother," so to speak. Normally, as a man grows up, there is a bonding with the mother, then the break with the mother. He breaks with the father when he discovers another male father, a coach, a hero, a mentor.

Finally, after Parsifal has worked at the castle and been trained there by Gournamond, he takes off his mother's homespun clothes. Finally he has an authentic male relationship and his own male identity! Gournamond teaches him how to wear the armor and ride the horse and especially how to stop it. Heretofore, he did not know how to stop the horse, how to set limits to his own phallic drives. Most important, Gournamond teaches him the crucial question to be asked at the appropriate time: "One day you are going to come upon a great castle, bigger than my castle. It will be the Grail castle, and when you get there, remember only to ask one question."

The one big question

His mother had told him to ask no questions. The good father says, ask the right question. The right question is, "Whom does the Grail serve?"

What, in other words, is the journey for? What is the goal of all this? It is the question we ask of the Twelve Step program: What's it for? What is recovery for? We have to ask this of all aspects of American civilization. All this efficiency and productivity, what's it for? To achieve what goal? And then what? That's the Grail question. It forces us to the ultimate. Then what? So what?

So what if Tom, Dick, or Harry is president? Then what? The question leaves us in perpetual dissatisfaction. It leads to what the Gospel would call the kingdom question. The question of the absolute. Where is the king of kings? Who is the final king we serve? This question never lets us be satisfied with smaller kings or smaller tribes. Whom does the Grail finally serve?

Therapists must want to ask sometimes, "What is my psychological work for?" I have therapist friends who tell me, "People have been coming to me and paying thousands of dollars and I sometimes want to ask that question, but it sounds too spiritual."

"What are you doing all this for?"

"Well, to improve my marriage."

That's good, but that's a minor grail. When you improve your marriage, what's that for? So you'll die and live happily ever after? Okay, but why do you want to live happily ever after? Those questions come to light only in the presence of the Grail. In some ways we don't know how to ask the question until we have seen the Grail unveiled. We don't dare to imagine or ask about the Absolute until we have first tasted it. The Grail invites us to the Grail. Grace tells us that there *is* grace, and anything less than grace will no longer satisfy.

Gournamond tells Parsifal he is to respect and protect all women. The same thing his mother told him. But — and this is a big but — the godfather teaches him that under no conditions is he to seduce a woman or be seduced by her.

Where did that come from? One answer is that such seduction would end the journey. Once he got a woman to bed, that would be it. He'd have arrived. What could there be more than to bed her down? Isn't that the Grail?

Wouldn't you know it — Parsifal starts losing interest in the training. He starts wanting to leave the castle. He tells his godfather that he's starting to worry about Mom. He hasn't called her for months. It's a major anima attack.

Gournamond tries to talk him into staying longer. "There's more I need to teach you." But a young man in the grip of an anima attack is helpless, even in relation to his father-figure. At New Jerusalem, some of the boys were like sons to me. The only thing that broke their loyalty to me was when they fell in love with a girl. They would immediately become inseparable from her. Then they would call up later and apologize because they didn't come and see me. At that point the young man will reject the father-figure, abandon him. The new fire has to be followed.

So Parsifal sets off back to his mother. But he comes upon another castle. First there was the masculine castle of Gournamond; now he comes to the castle of Blanche Fleur, White Flower.

The guy finally meets the girl

What a lovely name for the feminine castle: White Flower, the virginal one who will accept him into her virginal purity. This is the *anima* encounter. His soul is lured, attracted, and entrapped. Here before him is his other side, his twin, the image of the beloved. Believing he has found his wholeness with her, he goes to bed with her.

What's going to happen? Is he going to obey his godfather? He goes to bed with her, but — I'm afraid few people will be able to believe this today — he lies with her, nose to nose, toe to toe, but he does not seduce her or allow himself to be seduced by her. They just lie there, looking into one another's eyes.

She is henceforth his lady, his soul, his inspiration. Older Catholics remember, even though we don't say it much anymore, the Litany of the Blessed Virgin Mary, which included such exotic titles as "Mystical Rose," "Tower of Ivory," "Cause of Our Joy," "Singular Vessel of Devotion," "Ark of the Covenant." That's all Grail! All these titles apply to the eternal feminine symbolized in Mary. That's the power of the ideal woman, the vessel that holds our hope. Cause of our joy, cause of our hope — the one who will lead us. Pure love of a good woman can call forth immense and endless idealism in a man.

Parsifal stays there with her; we don't know how long. The impression is that maybe it was just one ecstatic night when he lay with her head to toe but did not have intercourse.

The quest, however, still has power to call him. So we are here watching a man becoming whole. He can go to the castle of the good father, Gournamond, and he can go to the castle of the beautiful White Flower, and he can leave both of them. Now he is finding his power inside himself. He finds his maleness and his femaleness inside himself. He does not need to stay in either castle.

This myth relates profoundly to celibacy. There is no way a man can be celibate unless he walks this journey. Without this kind of interior journey, unless he meets the inner woman and deepest man, he will keep looking for it out there.

The soul will be extroverted, acted out, and lost. He must also "act in," and pay the price of a difficult interior journey.

The incomparable Grail experience

The quest calls Parsifal on, and he leaves the second castle. He wanders through the woods and comes upon a fisherman. This may be a Christ image. Or just a man dipping into the unconscious. We don't know. The fisherman points him toward a hidden castle, surrounded by a moat and drawbridge, and tells Parsifal what direction to go. He crosses the moat on his horse, crosses the drawbridge, and (in most of the accounts), once he crosses the drawbridge, the gate snaps closed behind him.

Here we have a contained Grail experience. It's a moment in life that feels like an insertion into life, as if it came from somewhere else. It's the New Jerusalem descending in the twenty-first chapter of the Book of Revelation. It's not like the rest of life. It's a once-upon-a-time event. It's not mere chronological time anymore (*chronos*), but time as significance, threshold, and epiphany (*kairos*). It's a whole new room that you never lived in before; it's when time stopped at the death of your mother, the birth of your child, your first love touch, and the first experience of the holy. Both space and time are different here.

As I describe the Grail experience, it will help if readers can recall the moments of Grail experience they have had. These are very hard to describe. The best things can't be talked about. Most often it happens to little boys, four and five years old, and usually there was no godfather around to tell what it meant, or how to savor it, or live with it.

Then it recurs often in the teenage years, often associated

with the first love affair. He feels like he is floating. He feels like life finally makes sense.

In the Grail castle, the hero is in the realm of immortal images. Everything seems to shine. Everything seems to work and make sense. It is Jesus in the Temple at twelve, in his father's house, where he knows he is secure. It is not an intellectual belief system anymore; he knows in his body, his gut and heart. He could probably even measure it in terms of body sweat, or body calm and centered-ness. This is what Jesus would finally call the kingdom. It's whatever word we choose for the ultimate experience, when we know radically that everything is okay, no matter what's going wrong, *it's okay*.

Often this happens in the midst of great abuse. I remember a young man who was physically beaten by his father. He went back to his room after the beating. Then he literally went out the window. He was going to jump from the window in despair at being beaten by his dad, and it was there and then he had the Grail experience. There, all of a sudden, he knew things were radically all right. He was a Puerto Rican youth and he spent the rest of his life searching for that moment again, for the good father who revealed himself after the beating by the bad father.

This is the first numinous experience that opens our eyes. It only needs to happen once. It happened to Julian of Norwich, the English mystic, one May 8, and she lived off of it for the rest of her life. She tried to describe it in her writings, which she called "Showings." That night, God showed her his heart. Nothing more happened. People such as Angela Merici, who founded the Ursulines, and Junipero Serra had religious experiences at seventeen and eighteen that told them what they were going to do, and neither of them did it until they were fifty-five.

From eighteen to fifty-five was the unfolding. Then, when it happened at fifty-five, they knew what they were born for. When that moment comes, it is great and it is all synchronicity. We know then that grace is at work and we are not manufacturing our own lives.

The terrible thing about staying too long in heroic consciousness is that we may think we're building the tower alone. That's the dark side of the hero. "I've got to do it." The pagan myths are that: I've got to do it. There is still the sense of the gods whipping in and out of their lives. But what emerges in the great faith traditions is the radical sense of grace. I can't do it; all I can do is *be ready* and *awake.*

Jesus constantly told people to be awake (see Mark 13:33–37). That's all the hero can do — is be ready. If we set out to plan and create our own heroic path, it will be no more than our own heroic path, what we call ego. That's the false hero, finally the anti-hero. The real heroic path is created for us. We know someone else is preparing it. We can almost use this as a criterion in spiritual direction to see where someone's at: When people are still building all the doors and other parts, when they're still trying to make it happen, then we know they're still early in the journey (pure ego-consciousness is in control).

When, finally, we are able to be open — and it takes work to be open — and when we can be awake — and it takes work to be awake, too — then we are on the true heroic journey of what we usually call the saint.

What evolves is less and less control. We sense that, more and more. Someone else is for us, more than we are for ourselves. All we can do is get out of the way. We realize that this is a radically benevolent universe and it is on our side despite the absurdity, despite the sin, despite the pain and dead ends. It will feel more like letting go than taking on. Maybe that is why it is hard to accept.

This first numinous experience is probably possible only after one has positively experienced maleness and femaleness. Gournamond and the Red Knight represent the positive male experiences, and the nameless woman and White Flower represent positive femaleness. Now one is a human person and ready to "make love" to the wholeness that is God.

Grail King and another guy

The castle is the image of the whole self. A big house with all the rooms — the turrets, towers, bedrooms, kitchens, dungeons: It is the whole house where the totality is held together.

Parsifal finds two kings inside the Grail castle, not just one. First, there is the Grail King, whom he sees only for a moment, in a room in the center of the castle, while a procession is coming out the door. The only description given of the Grail King by Parsifal is that he is "the most beautiful man he ever beheld." Clearly a God-image. The door is shut after the procession comes out, and Parsifal never sees the Grail King again. But he cannot forget what he saw.

In the outer chamber of the castle is the wounded king or the Fisher King. His name is Amfortas, or Infirmity — without strength. The two kings are the two parts of his own soul, the godly part and the broken part. The godly king is the one who will hold the castle together, that part of him that always says yes to God, that accepts the Gospel; the broken king is the part that feels tragically obsessed, neurotic, and sick. Both parts are in him. He must not only discover his true self, but bring the two kings, the two parts, together.

The experience of God is always an experience of totality. There is enough room for everything, a universal spaciousness. Nothing need be excluded. Everything is allowed space by God. That is why, in our later years, we can become holy fools. The holy fool, like the trickster, can play with the dark side of things and not be threatened. This is hard to do when one is young and building the tower and in need of clear definitions.

Anything can be a Grail

Anything can become a Grail if it opens us up. Anything can become a symbol of universal truth if it leads us to ask: Who made it? Where did it come from, and why? Why is there anything? This is simple contemplation.

Let me tell you a true story. A family with a four-year-old son had another baby. They brought the new baby home and put it in its crib. The older boy said to his parents, "I want to talk to my little brother." They said okay. He said, "I want to talk to him alone." That surprised them, but they went outside. They did, however, stop to eavesdrop at the door. The little boy went up to the crib and said: "Quick, tell me who made you, tell me where you came from. Quick, I'm beginning to forget."

It should not be hard to believe this story. We already know who we are. All we have to do is uncover and awaken it. It's not a matter of getting the soul saved, but allowing the soul to emerge. The soul already knows we came forth from God and will return to God and that we are beloved.

Remember William Wordsworth's "Intimations of Immortality"? I think he is saying the same thing, but in unforgettable language:

> Our birth is but a sleep and a forgetting:
> The Soul ... cometh from afar:
> Not in entire forgetfulness,
> And not in utter nakedness,
> But trailing crowds of glory do we come
> From God who is our home:
> Heaven lies about us in our infancy!
> Shades of the prison-house begin to close
> Upon the growing boy ...
> The youth, who daily farther from the East
> Must travel,
> Still is nature's priest.

All this is symbolized by Jesus going into the desert and getting rid of "the prison house." Once we get the superficialities out of the way, the divine will always show itself. It's just a matter of time and choice.

But we must realize the qualitative difference between three minutes and thirty minutes, three days and thirty days. The issue is how much we are willing to wait and listen and trust.

In the classic vision quest of the Native Americans, the young man would go into the wilderness and find a spot — he did not keep wandering — and wait. He could not come back to the tribe until he had acquired his name and his vision. His name was given him by the spirits, who told him essentially who he was. It seems similar to the Christian name we chose for ourselves at Confirmation — a name we heard somewhere, a name we know is really who we are, a name we don't have to apologize for — at least that's the theory if not always the practice.

So many men fail to distinguish between a job and a vocation. If they do examine the difference, they realize that what they had all their lives was a job but what they want is a vocation — something that gives them a vision not of part of the castle but of the whole castle, some arrangement by which their work names who they are.

Not everyone has the luxury of achieving this. My father's generation never asked that question. My dad once said: "I didn't know I was supposed to enjoy my job." I think he found the Grail by faithfulness. He went to the Atchison, Topeka, and Santa Fe Railroad after he left the farm, and he never missed one day of work in thirty-five years. His loyalty and love were, of course, another path, another Grail.

Yet it remains only a desire in most men's souls today, to find their vision, what they were created to do, what they want to do, even if it doesn't earn as much money. If we are not willing to ask the economic question, to take a decrease in salary, for example, we are not really serious about going on the quest. That's why Jesus told the fishermen apostles, "leave your nets" — and that was the only livelihood they had (Matthew 4:19–22).

Family and job often keep us from the quest. They're the most sacred things in most of our lives, and often it's the most sacred things that hold us back. "Leaving the boat and their father, they followed him" (4:22).

Amfortas, the stricken king, cannot live because of his wound, but he cannot die because of the Grail. He lives in the castle, close to the Grail, but he is still sick and removed from it. He's caught in the middle. Many will recognize this predicament at once: We cannot live because of our wound (the tragic flaw at the center that seems to be keeping us from our life), but we cannot die because of our unfinished dream.

The Grail says that there is still something there — radical grace — and that there is something good at our core, that life is okay; it is the universal presence of the risen Christ. It will not let us die, it will not let us hate ourselves, it will not let humanity self-destruct, despite all the crucifixions.

The entire kingdom surrounding the castle is a wasteland, a stricken society in which nothing will grow. As T. S. Eliot describes it in his classic work "The Wasteland," it is a heap of broken images. The images are not working anymore. Their meaning is not breaking through to us anymore.

As long as things remain in the unconscious, we cannot make sense of them. They need to become visible in the conscious world. We see our soul in images. We need to search for the image in which we can see our soul. Then we will know why that image names and stirs us. That will be the image to carry us through to Spirit. If it leads us into grief, we have to go there. If it leads into anger, we have to go there. If it leads to a broken heart, we have to go there. If it leads to desire and ecstasy, great.

The need for erotic uplift

The Fisher King's wound is in his genitals, which makes him, as we say, incapable of action. He has lost the meaning of erotic instinct. The erotic is not primarily about sex; eros is about life. Days when we are not erotic are when we just don't care, are not motivated. When we give a damn, we are filled with eros.

Of course, at those same times we are also charged up sexually. If we are alive, we are alive in every way. When we're dead, we're dead — not in love with anybody or anything. "God, I don't want to bother being a human being. I don't have the energy for it." Thanatos as opposed to eros, death wish over life force. Eros is simply life energy. A good word for it is "juice." What soul work is about is how to wait for the juice: how to be open to it when it comes, how to recognize it when it's there, and how to let the images lead us to it.

It is clear that the kingdom will not be reclaimed until the Fisher King is healed. Until the head is healthy, the family or institution will not be healthy. We all share one another's sickness. We thought we made a great discovery some years ago about the dysfunctional family, but Christianity knew it already. We're all carriers. You're carrying the unlived life of your dad and the unlived life of your mother. And that's okay. The church's word for that was original sin. We're all carrying around this big brokenness that makes us yearn and hurt and desire. To *ache* for our own mother and father (to "honor" them) is also to ache for our own wholeness and to weep over our own wasteland. The wound is the way through. The only way through to the Big Picture.

Parsifal reaches the center of the Grail castle. The central room is called the Grail chamber. The door opens and he sees, amid a great light coming from inside, a beautiful man. From the center a grand procession is coming out. He just observes it. In the midst of a great religious or Grail experience, all we can do is observe. We know we're not creating it, that it is coming from somewhere beyond us.

That's the experience of grace. It's not self-generated. It's normally not an experience of our self-importance. The message is, rather, that there's something bigger beyond us. Our story is part of a much bigger story. The ego shrivels; we know we are only a grain of sand in the universe. But the exciting news is that it's okay. There is no need to run to our therapist whining, "I'm just a grain of sand." Finally we are happy to be a grain of sand. It's a liberation *from* self — the freedom that defines the Christian, as opposed to the mere "freedom-to-choose" that defines a liberal.

Young man with a sword

The first one out of the Grail chamber is a young man with a sword. In mythology that sword has both a positive and negative connotation. The positive meaning is the ability to be decisive and discriminating, the faculty to say no and yes and move ahead with life. This is here and this is there, everything orderly. It clarifies, helps us understand. It does not deny feeling, but it separates out the feeling from the issue so we can deal logically and effectively with it.

Unless Parsifal has the discipline and detachment to know what the God encounter asks of him, he will almost certainly abuse and misuse it. Witness so much junk religion today: God experiences that lack any human containers, boundaries, or discernment.

The sword also carries a negative connotation: killing. And indeed, something does have to be killed: the dark side, the shadow self. For a man to be born, a boy has to die, and that is a killing. It is painful. Mystical theology never shrinks from talking about the slaying of the dragon. In this context the sword expresses the healthy warrior, the spiritual side of the warrior.

The negative, too, must be presented to consciousness. This is the second figure to come out of the Grail chamber: a young man with a bleeding lance.

Recall the gargoyles on the corners of the temple. If we don't confront the negative, it will attack us. It will often destroy us. Experts think this image of the sword was probably added during a period of more muscular Christianity. Blood = life = soul = Christ = liberation = sacrifice = cross. Put them all together: That's the path, and it is symbolized by a bleeding lance.

Blood is the symbolic essence of power and the price that must be paid for power. The drinking of the blood symbolizes the taking of the divine essence within the self. We're not in the left-brain, logical sphere anymore. This is the world of sacred image. There is no adequate way to make it neatly conceptual; we're in the realm of non-rational knowing, of images that touch the soul at a deeper level than the left brain. We are in the temple of transformation.

Next in the procession from the castle comes a young woman carrying the Holy Grail. The earlier accounts had it unveiled; later legends said veiled. Notice, first, that it is carried by a woman. The soul, the feminine, the anima offers spirit to the ego. Parsifal is the ego, the woman is the soul, the Grail is the Spirit. Here we have them all working together.

At the castle, a great table is set. At first, Parsifal simply observes, he does not act. He finally eats, but that is his only action. Instead, he is acted upon in body and especially in spirit. Finally, he is led to his room by servants who undress him, bathe him, and put him to bed.

This is almost baptismal imagery. Bathing in water is not just Christian symbolism. Once I had the opportunity to visit the River Ganges and saw the Hindus coming down in hordes to bathe, doing their daily baptism. I could see how these people understood spirituality. The Indian people are almost obsessed with spirituality, almost to the degree we are obsessed with materiality. For good and for ill in both cases.

In all of this Parsifal forgets the crucial question: "What is all this for?" Instead, he just gets into the religious experience. He can't wait to run back to the prayer group and tell them he was baptized in the Spirit. He's just waiting to go home on Thursday and tell his wife he did the vision quest or the soul quest. He gives away his gold before it is gold, so he doesn't have gold. He doesn't know what the question is, although he's within it.

That's the way God entices and seduces us. This is an initiation rite. It's what the Mount Tabor transfiguration experience was for the apostles so they'd be ready to recognize the real Resurrection when it came. Furthermore, it will be remembered and understood only later. It is interesting, finally, that the first two figures were male, but the Grail bearer was a woman.

In the morning, our hero awakes alone. He's naked. He's bathed. He leaves the castle, and the drawbridge snaps closed behind him.

The problem of living with grace

Now the experience is over and he is back in the forest, back in the world as he knows it. He has been touched by God in such a way that only God will do from now on. He is trapped in the truth. He has experienced the absolute, and the relative will never again totally satisfy him. He aches for God. The aching now becomes the seeking.

We want to say, "It's not fair, God, that you don't come and take back the heart you first wounded. How dare you flirt with me. How dare you seduce me." Thus, after the Grail experience, our lives are driven in perpetual dissatisfaction. We are dissatisfied with everything: with the church, with self, with America. No matter whom they elect president, we'll be unhappy. This is a radical, aching dissatisfaction: Ordinary life will never again be good enough.

God is henceforward both perfectly hidden and perfectly revealed in everything. Most of the time the divinity feels more hidden than revealed. Once the Styrofoam cup becomes a Grail, even though the rest of your life it looks like a Styrofoam cup, you know it is also a golden cup. What drives you crazy is that you can't tell anybody, and they all think it is just a Styrofoam cup. After the Grail experience, the ordinary has forever become extraordinary.

A peak experience can be disconcerting. You wonder if it is a gift. You wonder if you're grateful for it. You wonder because you don't fit in anymore. You live the rest of your life at a tilt. You're skewed, off-center. What does Jesus say — "The world will hate you." You can't get excited about the things people get excited about. You don't believe them anymore. You know they're all shadow and disguise. Why does everybody fall in love with the shadow and disguise? Don't they know?

Our ingenuity in running away from the Grail is endless. Because we want to stop being tortured. But God is setting the ambush. That's the spiritual journey. That's the Hound of Heaven. That's the heart of the Bible.

It's not about being perfect. It's about getting involved in this great wrestling match. We get wounded in the hip, like Jacob, and we limp the rest of our life, but we're not handicapped by the limp. We are utterly confused but we are not confused by our confusion. We can live with our confusion now because, behind it all, *we know.* We see the fearsome state of the planet, but we're not frightened anymore by our fear.

Does it sound like double-talk? It isn't, but it sounds like it. When one gets into Grail language, it all sounds like paradox. Everyone wants to pull us back to the first language of logic, law, and tower building. But we know we can't go anywhere with that. We have jumped off the tower. Once Parsifal has seen the Grail — even though he returns over the moat and leaves the castle — he is radically different ever after.

Not that we remember the Grail forever after. We sin. We betray. We abort our own truth. We act absolutely contrary to our values and beliefs. We are hypocritical, lazy, lustful, and all the rest. But we are also trapped in the truth.

We know we are not any better for having seen the Grail. I have seen my shadow too many times. I don't live half the things I teach. But I still have to teach them because I still know they're the truth. As Jeremiah says, it burns within us (Jeremiah 20:9). We know it's the truth, even though we can never live up to it. Henceforward the only sin would be to deny that it *is* the truth. Trying to live up to it is the rest of the Grail journey.

Now the quest is real because the Grail is real.

Chapter 6

The spiral that teaches _____

When Parsifal leaves the Grail castle, the drawbridge closes behind him. This experience is like coming down from a high and returning to reality.

What follows, with minor variations in the different Grail accounts, is a long period of aimless wandering. Again and again our hero longs to go back and find his mother. At other times he longs to find Blanche Fleur. He is constantly subject to random moods and thoughtless, non-contemplative actions. He is frantically doing this and that, all business but getting nowhere.

There is, at this stage, no apparent quest, because there are no apparent questions. He has not heard on a deep level the question life is asking. His situation is similar to that of the Old Testament Israelites wandering in circles through the desert for forty years.

That forty is symbolic of the midsection of most of our lives. The point is: Even after we have been granted the Grail experience, we can forget it again as we get bogged down in our lives. There is a circular but spiral character to life. What many religions call the inexorable wheel of dying and rising. Of remembering and forgetting, winning and losing, suffering and enjoying. The Grail search can get tossed about at the mercy of life's spinning wheel of fortunes.

In Parsifal's wanderings there are many minor incidents. He encounters many lesser characters. They are simply the symbols of what we need along the way. The underlying trust that sustains our hero at such times is: When you need it, it's going to be there. It's a benevolent universe, and Parsifal is at home.

In George Lucas's *Star Wars* trilogy, for example, a little gnome occasionally appears in the woods. This is the voice we need to hear at a particular time, and the hope is that we will have the freedom and wisdom to hear it. Several from the Grail story are regarded as pivotal.

Three women

He meets, for example, three significant women.

First, there is the woman who has not laughed for six years. A woman without any joy. Yet, when she meets Parsifal, she learns to laugh. She cheers up because, as she says, he is the best knight in the world. This seems to be the positive encounter with the feminine. Indeed, it is a mutual positive encounter. She is able to call him the best knight in the world, and he is able to make her laugh.

This positive mood seduction is a gift along the journey. It keeps us going for another few months. It is not the Grail, but there is nothing wrong with it. It represents the little joys of our ordinary lives that keep us going — the beer and pizza with friends on Tuesday night.

There is nothing wrong with human joy, nothing wrong with little gifts. All of life can't be the Grail every day around the clock. Someone has remarked that 95 percent of life is "Mickey Mouse." Pile upon pile of nonsense. Most of the work we do — bureaucracy, filling out forms, mowing the lawn — tempts us to ask: What does this have to do with the kingdom? In the middle of this Mickey Mouse routine, however, fall occasional pearls of great price if we are awake to notice them.

Even in the Grail quest we find a lot of Mickey Mouse. What's archetypal about that, one may ask. Alas, most of life isn't archetypal.

It's not accidental that in a number of the world's

languages the word "spirit" is used to describe alcohol. Everyone is aware of the sufferings abusive drinking brings into so many lives, yet we dignify alcohol with exalted names like spirit or spirits. There is something significant there. The place of the wound is the place of the breakthrough. The place of the pain is the place of the promise.

Even Jesus was using the same analogy when he asked his apostles, "Can you drink of the cup?" The cup he describes is both the cup of ecstasy and the cup of suffering. These women Parsifal meets seem to signify different cups.

The second woman he meets is the sorrowing woman who lets him know the pain he has caused by killing her knight.

He has, as the story unfolds, killed many knights along the way, and sent others back wounded to Arthur's court.

One way to interpret the latter is as an integration of Parsifal's own demons, as it were, sending them back to the Round Table. Mythologically they're not so much a killing as an encountering, so each one is a recognizing of a part of himself, confronting it, and accepting it as part of the package of his life.

Killing dragons is a feature of all mythologies. It's always the same image, the feathered serpent, a creature that does not even exist on the earth. It is a symbol of something that, first of all, crawls on the ground, yet has wings — a flying serpent. What the myth makers were putting together, obviously, was the earth and the heavens. It comes from the earth, yet it flies — that fascinates us. The duality begs to be overcome.

In the Genesis account of the seven days of creation, it says of the third day that it was very good, and of the fourth, fifth, and sixth days that what happened was very good. But it does not say on the first and second days that it was very good. Check it out! See Genesis 1:3-8.

On the first day, darkness was separated from light, and the story does not say it is good. We are reminded that the work of religion is precisely to put darkness and light back together — that is what we are trying to do when we deal with the shadow. It is not good when darkness and light are thought to be totally separate.

The second day is to separate heaven from earth, separate the wings from the lizard, the swan from the dog, what is heavenly from what is earthly. The dragon always puts those two back together — heaven and earth.

Genesis does not say the second day was good because it is not good to separate heaven from earth. The religious experience, the Grail experience, is to realize there is only one world — and it is supernatural. It is a mistake to divide the world into the natural and the supernatural. Yet that was the theology most of us grew up with.

There is only one world, one history, and it is God's — and also ours. Once we realize that, everything is different. Trees start shining and we do not have to go to church to discover God. There is only one world — supernatural — and it is not good when light is separated from darkness, and heaven from earth. Good *"re-ligio"* binds it all back together.

We return to Parsifal. The sorrowing woman is sorrowful not just because of the suffering he has caused, not even for killing her knight, but also because he was in the Grail castle and did not ask the Grail question.

She asks him his name, and for the first time he knows it: Parsifal. Previously, he was always "Dear Son." It is only when the woman confronts him with the pain he has brought into the world, by living stupidly and asking the wrong questions, by killing people needlessly, by not integrating his own shadow but sending it back to King Arthur's court — it is only then that he learns his name. He finally grows beyond Momma's boy.

Only grief and suffering will bring us to consciousness. People normally do not cross to the state of high self-awareness except by fording the river of suffering.

Inflation and pride will normally keep us in ego-unconsciousness (where we try to fix and control everything because we think our limited understanding is really understanding). We call it living in illusion. The uninitiated boy lives in a state of inflation that has been called "infantile grandiosity." Until that is deflated, he does not know his name.

That, by the way, is the wisdom of the Twelve Step programs. The deflation of the alcohol experience has taught many men and women their name. Finally they know who they are, not just who they're supposed to be in the public image. It is always a humiliating experience to find out how ordinary you are. This is similar to discovering one's enneagram number: very humbling! And if it is not humiliating, you haven't got the right number. If people are all excited about being Fours, for example, they are not Fours. If you're a Four, and you see how stupid it is to be a Four, you don't want to be a Four. Or any enneagram number, for that matter.

It is usually the feminine that leads the man into his grief. She reminds him of the pain he has caused. That's why celibates live such a deprived, or even dangerous, life: They lack the truth-speaker a married man has. They do not have that feminine soul right there saying we have not spoken honestly for six months, have not been our real selves for a year.

It is very clear in the Grail story that it is the women who constantly keep Parsifal growing up. They force him to face his dark side.

In all fairness, that should also be a man's role vis-à-vis his wife. And all too often, men do not rise to the occasion. The feminine also needs to be challenged by male reality.

If the man does not face the pain of things, what Virgil called the *lacrimae rerum,* the tears of things, he will remain forever what John Lee calls a "flying boy." Left to himself, he is dangerous. He is unreal. He certainly won't touch anybody at any significant level. The young man must be taught to weep.

The third woman Parsifal meets is the hideous woman. She is sometimes called the sorceress. Right when he is in the middle of a big meal with his friends, for example, and trying to make a good impression, this hideously ugly woman rides in on a mule. In the middle of the meal, in front of everybody, she recites all his sins.

It's the accusing woman, the witch. She tells what he did wrong, what he did not do in the Grail castle. She accuses him. And remember: That's the biblical term for Satan — the accuser. It represents the inner, negative voice that is constantly accusing us. It repeats, "You're not good enough.... You haven't done it right."

Watch that negative feminine

Parsifal is now walking the razor's edge; how does one confront the shadow and yet refuse to be condemned by it (identify with it). The shadow voice reveals to Parsifal his dark side. She tells us we don't do anything right. Many men live their whole lives this way, under the accusing voice of the negative feminine. Maybe it's their mother's voice, maybe it's their wife's voice, maybe their own voice. In any case, everything is the man's fault. The witch is riding her broom.

I have counseled many people who were tortured by this voice. They usually have the same, self-loathing line: "I'm a dumb shit, I can't do anything right." Something like that. Then it becomes a self-fulfilling prophecy. They make a victim of their lives and they believe the lie. They believe the shadow, identify with it.

We should never *identify* with the shadow. It is, at best, part of the truth. In reality, that's the source of much that is evil: people who think they *are* their shadow selves. These people beat themselves down mercilessly for what they have done wrong and identify with their guilt and shame.

When we confront the shadow, the response is usually not anger but sadness. Most men have days of deep sadness, and these are usually a sign that our psyche has, in the recent past, confronted some of our dark self. We get a glimpse of how broken, how poor we are. The heroic male response is to attack it, fix it, deny it, or dramatically share it. The saint merely weeps over it, until its lesson is learned.

The saint is one who has faced the dark self and is no longer shocked by it. That's why saints don't get depressed. They have confronted the enemy and forgiven him. It's okay to be a poor man or a poor woman.

Now we are back to the Gospel. If there is not that embrace of poverty (the shadowy and shamed part of the self), the willingness to be one of the little ones, the least of the brothers and sisters, we will always live in dissatisfaction and grief that we are not good enough. Once we know the poverty of our condition is okay, and maybe even *the way,* then we do not need to fight it.

Some of the angriest men I have met are those who feel their mother took away their father's joy, took away their father's manhood, beat him down. Their mother constantly nagged him. Along with the anger at the hideous mother, there is usually a massive distrust of women. Such men fear intimacy because they are determined never to let a woman henpeck them the way their mother did their father.

This makes it impossible for a man to entrust himself to a woman. Until that is grieved through, talked through, carried through, he can never enter a healthy relationship with a woman. He will keep laying on her his own history with regard to his mother.

Black Knight

At this point, Parsifal meets the character called Vassal, the Black Knight. The grievous problem of racism makes it difficult for us to use "white" and "black" for good and evil, but they are consistent terms in mythology and we have to ask why. Blackness symbolizes night when things are hidden and not seen; that's the shadow world in which there is no consciousness or light or sight.

People of color have suffered from this terminology all around the world. The darker a person's skin is, the easier it seems to project the unworthy part of our selves on that person. It has nothing to do with logic. In that awful sense we could say black people must be the chosen people — the scapegoats, the Christ images — because they bear the shadow projections of so much of the world.

I don't know why God allows such confusions, but it happens all around the world. I don't know why God allows such injustice; that's part of the mystery. It is part of the essentially tragic nature of life. Why should some people start off with such a negative handicap (although the Gospel would call it a head start!)?

The majority of those with white skin are oblivious — unaware they were born with some sort of silver spoon in the mouth. Most whites don't realize the system is skewed in their favor because of their color, or because they are American and male. It all just seems to work out for us white males of the West, so it's easier for us just to think we're smarter. Or maybe harder working. And maybe we have worked hard, but in any case our path was paved. We are, in worldly terms, the top of the pile. The whole world system is designed to feed and pamper us.

One reason I give these retreats to men who have the time and money to come to them is that we are the ones most in need of liberation. We are trapped at the top and must deconstruct from the top.

And the challenge for white males is to be willing to go back down. It is incumbent on us to let go of the power, prestige, and privilege the system grants. I have been in too many foreign countries to believe that white people work harder. I have seen the little campesinos of Latin America leave for the fields at six in the morning and not get back until dark. They work all day. Don't fall for the illusion that we deserve our wealth because we work harder. The poor world needs liberation from outer structures, and the overdeveloped world needs liberation from inner illusions.

Parsifal meets the Black Knight, who lives in a tomb, in a state of enchantment. A not-so-wise maiden tries to persuade him to kill the Black Knight, his shadow self. Fortunately, in the nick of time, he meets a wise old man, who tells him not to attack the Dark Knight, not to drive Vassal back into his tomb, but instead to invite him out and make peace with him. There you have it. Jung did not discover this, as many seem to think. They had discovered it in the eleventh and twelfth centuries.

We call it making friends with our shadow.

Insight into the shadow is perhaps the most significant breakthrough to understanding the real meaning of morality and of the moral quest. Jesus understood it and spoke of it in a number of parables, most clearly in Matthew 13. This is one of the most underquoted and underused parables of Jesus. "A man sows good seed in his field."

That's us. We were good Christian men. We went to church and did the right thing. We sowed good seed in our fields. But in midsummer we descend on the landowner and say, "I sowed good seed, but there are weeds growing amid the wheat. Where did the weeds come from?"

That's the typical question when we first discover we're hypocrites. We discover, for example, that, although we call ourselves pacifists, we're just as violent as the next one, only in a different way. We are, in fact, like the people we are against.

The man in the parable, at least, faces the shadow, recognizes the weeds in the field. He asks the master, "Should I go and pull the weeds?" But Jesus says, no, do not pull the weeds. Don't even think you can do it. If we pull out the weeds, we will pull out the wheat as well. So Jesus said to *"let them both grow together"* and at the end of time God would decide, would separate the weeds and wheat, would throw the weeds into the fire.

Why such a strange, paradoxical procedure? Because, basically, if we do otherwise, we will mess it up. We don't know what our gifts are and we don't know what our sin is. The spiritual journey teaches that, and it takes the whole journey to learn it. The enneagram teaches that. What we think is our gift when we're twenty turns out to be our greatest sin when we're forty. Those who are twenty should wait and see. What you ride on, what you build on when you're twenty, is what may destroy you later.

The shadow self, first of all, is not the evil self. It is, rather, the unacceptable self — that side of us that, for whatever reason, whether it be family or cultural or church reason, we do not want to present publicly. It does not reflect well on us to let everybody know, for example, that we read *Playboy* magazine. So no one knows we have a *Playboy* under the mattress. That's our shadow self. Sexuality is almost always in the arena of the shadow self, at least in the West.

Hypocrisy and other gray areas

The qualities, therefore, that we want to present to the outer world are the ones that reflect our desired self-image — and they are always balanced by their opposite, which lodge in the shadow.

The shadow self is always the scorned part of the self, which eventually must be allowed to return and teach us. That which is chosen *against* while building our tower (poverty, meekness, non-violence, simplicity) becomes the greatest lesson of the second half of life. We are actually *linked* to our shadow by our harsh judgments against it. Our shadow is not really our opposite as much as our *rejected twin* — to whom we are negatively bound, but bound nevertheless.

Mention has already been made of the pacifist who is convinced he is non-violent. He is only twenty-one, and we marvel at how quickly he grew up and faced his demons. And then we go to an activist meeting with him and we find the guy is filled with control needs.

His violence has taken a much more subtle form. He rejected the violent self, projected it onto Ronald Reagan or some other rogue, so he could hate someone besides himself, and that's how we usually deal with our shadow. We don't own up to it, deep down, but instead project it onto someone else.

Many feminists are doing that today. They fulminate against men, these pigs, all patriarchal types, all into authority and power. And then we visit their house and across their mantle they have a pantheon of sixteen different goddesses and gods, while rejecting one God who holds life together. Their split-up psyche is all over the place and it's no place. They are angry at power because they have not, perhaps, integrated and tamed their own power needs.

Our usual lame solution is to hate the shadow "over there." But we can't hate it over there; we can't deal with it over there; we have to confront it in here in ourselves, have to love it in here in ourselves. Everything we hate has to be re-invited, has to be made friends with.

It's futile to hate it over there, to point and say, men are the problem, poor people are the problem, blacks are the problem, Protestants are the problem, Catholics are the problem — anybody outside my group will suffice as the problem.

We all do it. We decide what we want to look like and then the rest goes underground. Growing up means taking the lid off, going inside the cave and making friends with the Dark Knight, with Vassal.

That task will take more humility, more time and more courage than any task in our lives. It will never stop. It just goes deeper and deeper as we learn to grieve over our sins, to weep over our silliness, our lives of inconsistency and contradictions. As Joseph said to his brothers, "You cannot come into my presence unless you bring your littlest brother with you" (Genesis 44:23).

The final stage of this descent is that of the fool. A young man who cannot cry is a savage, and an old man who cannot laugh is a fool. At the end, if we are lucky, we learn to laugh. The confrontation with the shadow is what teaches us to laugh at ourselves.

By contrast, the young boy building his tower can't laugh. Equally tragic, he can't cry. He can't feel pain for the world, because he is too serious. He has to do what he has to do to get saved, to become holy, to be correct. There is neither time to smell the flowers nor to laugh at himself nor to cry over the pain of the world. He is busy on the tower, trapped in an excess of spirit and a lack of soul.

The shadow self is usually a combination of feelings, thoughts, words, and images. I directed a conference for a large group of men in Switzerland. There is no cleaner country in the world. It is the most antiseptic place imaginable. I dared a friend to find any garbage, and after six days we had not seen any. Now here's the point. The Swiss retreat was going fine until I used the phrase, "full of shit." That was shocking to them. We, of course, don't say it all the time, either, but it's not shocking for us, but they actually found it offensive.

The connection is obvious. The self-image of the Swiss is clean. Their world is clean. Cleanliness is the ideal. And following the rules. I walked a foot over the median on a Sunday morning, at a time when where was no traffic, and a Swiss man walked over and scolded me. He wasn't a policeman, but I said, "Yes, sir." One follows the rules. That's how it remains the cleanest country in the world, an eternal postcard.

It's so perfect, in fact, that it's suspicious. One finds oneself wondering, have they ever wrestled with their shadow?

No doubt they have. The point is not to put down the Swiss. Every culture has its own peculiar traits. So does every individual. We each decide how we want to look. How we will look good to people we like and want to like us. All the rest goes underground: our uncivilized desires and feelings, everything we do not want to be. Everything we would like to be but do not dare. Everything we don't want others to know about us. Even everything we don't want to know about ourselves. We all have our secrets.

We live in a narcotized culture in which people do not have much self-knowledge. There is nothing rewarding in knowing oneself. So everything nasty or unpleasant is conveniently denied or forgotten. There is the personal shadow, which I would call the flesh, the collective shadow, which I would call the world, and the archetypal shadow, which I would call the devil. I am not denying a personal devil here, but simply making a point — the world, the flesh, and the devil were always called the three invitations to evil.

The shadow always turns to us the same face we turn to it. If we love it, if we learn how to embrace it and forgive it — the mystery of the forgiveness of sin — it will forgive us. And deal gently with us. If we hate it and attack it and live in complete denial, it will attack indirectly and come back and get us by the back door.

In the spiritual life, nothing goes away. There is no heavenly garbage dump. It's all here, wherever we are. Everything belongs. Even forgiveness does not mean it goes away. It means we forgive it for being there, nothing more. Even our demons do not go away. As Robert Bly wisely said: You don't get rid of your demons, you just educate them.

Go ahead, talk to those demons

So, if we're wise, we start talking to our demons. We don't let them fool us about what's going on. We play the trickster. We become more sophisticated the older we get, but essentially most middle-aged men could go to confession now and say exactly what they said at nineteen. I recently read in a newspaper article that the personality at eighteen and the personality at forty are basically the same. The article conceded that we become more agreeable, more introverted, but we still are who we were.

Some may find this discouraging, for example, people

who go on a week's retreat in order to grow: They want to return home changed. That's fine, but it should be regarded as relative, especially in our 1990s American growth culture. All this talk about becoming whole, for example: No one talked that way until this century. We do not become whole. We just stay on the path and keep our eyes on the path. We focus on our goal and on ourselves, and then God does wonderful things. But all the while we are radically broken, even to the end. Hopefully our power to hurt others is decreased, as well as our need to punish ourselves.

Meanwhile, the prince of darkness tries to persuade us to remain unconscious. That's why he's called the prince of darkness and father of lies. Don't believe the truth about yourself, he whispers. The Paraclete is the "defense attorney" who defends us against this accuser (John 14:16ff.).

People with a repressed shadow — that is, with a heavy lid on their unlived life — have various giveaways. The first giveaway is that they will be heavy and serious and lacking a sense of humor. They see everything as a moral issue. Such people can't lighten up. This is especially true of Ones on the enneagram scale, for whom everything is monumental.

In reality everything is not monumental. Ninety-nine percent is Mickey Mouse. When we can face the shadow, we find this out and start loosening up. That's why the saints made so much of laughter. That's why the laughing woman provides an important encounter for Parsifal.

But the stern, moralistic guy who is being strangled by his shadow will go through life shaking his finger at what is wrong with everyone. I had professors like that, and I used to think, if this is what it's like to be a priest, I don't want to be one. That just can't be what it means to be Jesus in the world: to be so heavy and always judging and analyzing what is wrong.

The three great demons are fear, guilt, and anger. They dominate the lives of people who don't face their shadow. Fear has gotten away with a lot because we never recognized it as sin, even though Jesus warns against it more than anything else. We conveniently called our fears "prudence," necessary caution, self-defense until they finally became war and the national security state.

Guilt is interesting. Only people who need to feel worthy, who need the moral high ground, are obsessed with guilt. Once you know you're not all that important, just a little guy full of shit, you'll never waste another day on guilt.

People who live in the shadow tend to be aimlessly angry. They go about looking for someone to be angry with.

Catch the anger just as it starts, admit your anger, feel it, then laugh at it. That relaxes some of your egocentric grasp around your feelings.

The shadow is dangerous to the degree we are out of touch with it. In this light the church teaching about repentance, confession, and forgiveness of sin makes sense. The church is right, first of all, when it says to confess. Somewhere we have to say it. To admit it. "I'm Joe, and I'm an alcoholic." Or I'm a lustaholic, or a rageaholic. Just say it somewhere and bring it out of the darkness into the light. That's what we mean by making friends with the shadow. This is what the wise old man teaches Parsifal: *Don't kill Vassal. Bring him out and make friends with him.*

Most of the major crises in our lives are confrontations with our shadow selves. Invariably these are encounters that show us something about ourselves that we'd rather not see. They are, therefore, most painful, most distasteful, and we do everything we can to avoid them. We seek some cocoon of security and tell ourselves we're in good shape and therefore do not need any more "metanoia."

This metanoia is an elusive concept. It means a turning around. But this raises the question: How many times can one, or must one, turn around? Can't we just find the truth and stay with it? How can the Gospel ask for repeated, ongoing turning around?

The answer lies in our very human tendency to find another comfort zone. We faced one shadow, we're proud of our effort, and we think we're converted for good, so we rest on our laurels. Then the Gospel orders us again, turn around. Again? We're addicted to this self-image we worked so hard on and want to keep it. But we must let go of it. All right, so we build another castle and settle down. Then the Gospel says once more, turn around. It's always about letting go, a perpetual series of turning around.

We grow by giving up

Recently, I dreamed I was Indiana Jones. The whole night. I must have awakened five times, and every time I was in the middle of an adventure. I was flying heroically here and there and getting out of every crisis — talk about being inflated! Next thing, however, I'm standing naked in a pool of clean water like a fountain. The water is cascading over me, and I'm looking down and taking delight in my nakedness and in the water.

Then as I look at my feet, they turn into ugly club feet. The water that was washing me stops and instead my tears flow down over my club feet.

I woke up devastated. I was Indiana Jones all night, but then my unconscious reminded me that I have club feet. God gave me the message: You've got club feet and don't forget it. Our shadow self shows itself to us in our dreams. Therefore, we should cultivate our dreams. Even the erotic dreams. Often, the shadow comes to males in the form of the opposite sex. The point is not to get rid of it; we should observe it and then ask, what is the lesson?

In general, conservative personalities tend to *repress* too quickly, while liberals tend to *express* too quickly. Both approaches are counterproductive. Too quick expression — the "if it feels good, do it" syndrome — teaches us nothing. But we learn nothing from too quick repression, either. What we have to do is hold it in the middle. Don't repress, don't express, just stay there. Recall Parsifal lying in bed toe to toe and eyeball to eyeball with White Flower — not expressing, not repressing. That's when we learn. That's spirituality. That's wisdom. That's faith. That's discipline. That's patience. It's also hard.

If we plan only to be good and perfect, as we Ones try to be, according to our limited cultural religious ideal, too much of the internal vital energy is denied, too much of the instinctual energy that teaches and refines us. We become, instead, hateful and dangerous and we don't even know it.

A stark example is how dangerous even churchmen can be. Consider the tragedies religious people have inflicted throughout history. Consider the church's history here in the United States — the good Catholics coming here and participating in the genocide of the Indians. That's what happens when we do not understand the shadow side. All that happens is the "ungoodness" goes underground.

The church's primary failure might well be that it did not teach us *how to carry the dark side:* neither our personal darkness nor the darkness of history and institutions. Now it all comes back to get us!

Jesus was so much smarter. When the rich, flattering young man came up and said, "Good Master," Jesus retorted: "Why do you call me good?" (Mark 10:17–18). In other words, stop it. Stop flattering me. We must all watch flatterers who try to kiss up to us. Usually their flattery involves a denial of the shadow. They do not want to talk honestly. They refuse to talk, as we say, man to man. It is such manhood we are trying to discover here, a manhood that does not have to worry about being good. It just is, and that's all we should ask of it.

We need honesty and humility more than seeming heroism, but maybe that is heroism. This wrestling with the shadow is the game of life. It is what gives us personality. If we don't wrestle, we don't have a personality; there's nothing real or rugged or manly about us.

By contrast, there is a brand of smiling, sweet, good Christians who have pushed the shadow down to oblivion. They are not real; they are plastic people. One hopes they will come to a sense of their own diminishment, their own abandoned power. One example is the man who can't get angry with his wife. She's the witch in this scenario, always angry. He not only legitimates her anger but he deepens his own, because of his conviction that anger is wrong. In fact anger sometimes is appropriate and necessary.

John's Gospel tells us Jesus "made a whip of cords" (John 2:15). In other words, he *chose* to be angry. He walked into the temple, kicked over the table, and vented this deserved anger. It is the so-called "unworthy" emotions that ask the most of us and teach us the most.

God slips in occasional paradox

Mephistopheles, the Satan persona in Goethe's *Faust*, describes himself in this way: "I am part of that force which would do evil if I could, yet for some reason forever works the good." He goes on to complain that no one appreciates him, yet, "were it not for me, nothing good would ever happen." There's some truth there. It's the Trickster. It's the surprising way the truth gets at us.

Mephistopheles again: "You think I'm Satan, and yet I'm responsible for most of your good." This may cause some trouble at the level of dogma, but here we are talking on the level of soul. There is a place for the proper theological formulas, we know that, but we also know that the way it really happens is what we have to start talking about. Soul work needs to balance the pure clarity of spiritual forms.

M. Scott Peck quotes St. Thérèse of Lisieux: "If you are willing to serenely bear the trial of being displeasing to yourself, then you will be for Jesus a pleasant place of shelter." Peck, a twentieth-century psychologist, says this is one of the most profound pieces of psychological wisdom he has ever read. That's exactly what I see we will not do, says Peck. Especially religious people. We are not prepared to be displeasing to ourselves.

When I read that, I finally felt I understood the first line of the Sermon on the Mount: "Blessed are the poor in spirit." These are the little ones who know they are no big deal and are quite content being no big deal. These are the only people who are really free and invulnerable.

Blessed *are* the poor in spirit — you're home free. Jesus used the present tense. Yours *is* the kingdom of heaven (Matthew 5:3). You have it right now because you have no boundaries of prestige or power or righteousness or moral superiority or greatness or savedness to protect.

There is a right order to things. The confrontation with Vassal, with the shadow, could be contemplated and understood only after there has been a Grail experience — after there has been an experience of beloved sonship, unconditional acceptance, universal belonging. Until then, we do not have the guts to face the shadow. We cannot face the dark until we have seen the light.

To put it most simply, people who do not know God will continue, by and large, to live in illusion. People who are not walking a spiritual path will continue, by and large, to live a life of unconsciousness. They will not have that primal security that allows them to be insecure.

It is ironic that the people who receive most of the world's attention, and even adulation, are so busy living the unexamined life that they have no time or energy to do soul work. The politicians and actors and athletes, the movers and shakers haven't the time, or haven't chosen to walk an interior path. There is little reason to assume that more than a few of them have confronted their shadow. And those are the people by whom the world is being led, in country after country, in sphere after sphere of influence and endeavor. Mostly men. No wonder the women are worried.

We need a generation that will redeem the name of power, that will redeem the name of authority and redeem the name of wisdom. They will need to confront and tame the Dark Knight within. "Don't kill Vassal. Bring him out and make friends with him."

Chapter 7

To the heart of the Grail castle ____

Although the very best things cannot be talked about, and the next best things are almost always misunderstood, we must still try to come to terms with them. Perhaps the best we can do is touch them at tangents, catch glimpses of them by using examples and metaphors and myths.

The Grail is one such effort. In the Grail chamber lives the most beautiful man Parsifal has ever seen. Occasionally the door to the Grail chamber opens and a procession comes out, then returns.

We travel East for a kindred image. The inner sanctum in the center of Hindu temples is dark and empty. One enters through successive courts to the middle court. There, nothing more can be seen, or said. It is utter mystery, and all we can do is stand there in awe. We have moved beyond words, beyond understanding.

This, like the Grail chamber, is an image of God hidden in the depths of the unconscious.

Coping with the logic of life

Most people are trained and accustomed to live in their consciousness. That's how we succeed at what the world calls success. The only way we can build our tower is to cut off unconsciousness. It's too upsetting, too broad, too daunting, too ineffective to handle. In other words, it is too real, and humans can handle only a limited amount of reality. Consequently, in order to succeed, to make it through school, to build the tower, to please our parents, to please the church, we create the ego-container, the shell our conscious persona is most comfortable with.

The reason for building the container is to hold what is otherwise going to erupt as our lives grow and expand. The point is not just to keep building the container for its own sake; it's not meant to be the end product. For this reason, it is best to begin the container conservatively. It is best to begin with clear ego-identity and clear ego-boundaries — something strong enough to tell us who we are and who we are not, what's real and what is not.

The lines drawn at this stage are quite black and white. That's the straightforward tower, clear, well-defined. It is moving away from the ground and the earth and the messy. Such a project calls for clarity, order, law, structure, and a certain earnest spirit.

Therapists know how this works in real life. We cannot begin as liberals. It would be foolhardy to tell a four-year-old: Do what you want, anything goes, everything is wonderful. If we do this, they will quickly get hurt. Such license is one of the illusions of liberalism. No mythology and no tradition has ever said that one can begin with all the options open, with no clear boundaries. If the motto is to just let the ego float wherever it wants to float, it will float right into destruction and oblivion.

Building the container or tower constitutes the beginning of the hero's journey. Once it is built, he is likely to say to himself, I am this container. The trouble is, many people spend the rest of their lives defending that container because they spent so long building it that they think it is the sum of who they are. These are the men in the second half of life, still building their tower of self-image and security. The tower is now so high, it is very hard to get back to the muddy earth.

Hubris, nemesis, and ouch

In the middle of the Grail temple, we cannot talk. We are in the great unconscious, which is beyond words. The classical Greeks already saw the dangers lurking here. A primary characteristic of Greek tragedy is hubris. It is *the* sin. It is when the private self, the would-be hero — Parsifal — assumes for himself the qualities of the gods. The word for that is "inflation." It occurs when we think we are the totality, the center. When we identify with that most beautiful man. When we walk around thinking we're bigger than we are.

Whenever you have hubris in Greek tragedy, you will also have nemesis, the agent of justice and retribution. Any hero who overestimates his importance will surely face the vengeance of nemesis. He will, in short, fall, be defeated. The greater the illusion, the greater the humiliation; the higher the crawl, the farther the fall.

The more we think we are at the center of the Grail procession, the more we have to be pulled out of it and reminded of our small private selves. We are a part, not the whole. Even though this is called pride or hubris or inflation or sin or whatever, the paradoxical fact is that we must do it. That's not new teaching. That's the meaning of eating the apple. We must leave the garden. The garden is the totality, where it's all together as one. We must leave this center, this totality. In this particular world, in this fallen world, we must sin, be defeated, fall.

If we sit on the other side, that is, avoiding hubris in order to avoid nemesis, if we avoid the middle, avoid trying to be gods and greater than we are — the word for that is "alienation."

The reason this myth of the Holy Grail is considered an archetypal myth of Western civilization is because for the most part Parsifal is in a state of alienation. For the most part he is wandering around trapped in his little private self, unable to believe in any kind of relationship with or connection with the Living Center. We can't be *identified* with the Center — that's hubris. What religion gives us is a living *connection* with the Center. We are a part, not the whole. We are not *It*, but we are connected to It by bonds of love. Our word for that is salvation!

This protects us both from extraordinary guilt and extraordinary inflation. We know we are the least of the brothers and sisters, a little grain of sand. But, on the other hand, we are sons of the living God. What we do is keep moving in and out, back and forth. We will have the Grail experience, the inflating experience, and that will demand, sooner or later, its opposite. *Simul justus et peccator,* said Martin Luther; we are at the same time justified and sinners. Ernest Becker put it even more forthrightly: "We are gods who shit."

Yuppies and the fall from inflation

A wider source of worry is this yuppie generation that has grown up with so much inflation. With so many of their wants met. With the freedom. With the toys consumerism conferred on them. What will happen to them when their world gets real?

What are the suicide rates going to be twenty-five years from now? These people will not be able to deal with the nemesis. They will not be able to deal with old age. They will not be able to deal with the death of spouses or loved ones. Or with the loss of their job. If we live too long in the false Grail chamber, at what we think is the center, thinking we are the center, when the nemesis comes there will be almost no ability to deal with it and there will be hell to pay.

What a good guide does is teach us how to fall. Graciously. And even to trust the fall and realize that falling is a good way to learn.

Inflation is always followed by deflation. And after we have been deflated, we eventually get inflated again. That movement back and forth is what brings the unconscious into the conscious. We call the back and forth grace and sin. These are very traditional words, but psychologically they're very accurate.

You realize that you thought you were at the center, and that you misjudged it. You've taken yourself too seriously; you thought you were more important than you are. Then you fall. And that's the window, or door, through which the unconscious becomes conscious. That's called transformation, when the spirit erupts through our unconscious. In spiritual language it is called conversion.

There is no easy way to bring about conversion. Pain is needed to keep us from inflation. Otherwise we will wallow in that grandiose state of imagining how perfect and good and saved we are. The Twelve Step programs have gotten that right. They have identified the pain necessary to keep us from illusion. Without that pain, we would all go running to that false Grail chamber, to a false security system, a false naming of the self.

For some of us that false Grail chamber is the power job. For others, the prestigious education, perhaps the Ph.D. God is going to say: So what? Who cares? For some it's the role. Priest, for example. There's no more dangerous identification than a religious self-image.

The priest is endowed with the image and role of the magician, which makes him feel he has immediate access to the inner chamber. Most of us can still remember when the priest alone could open the tabernacle. What was that saying? The key to the inner chamber? That is dangerous for a young man. So dangerous that maybe the church should not ordain men under thirty-five. Priesthood goes to too many immature heads. And many never recover. They just keep opening the tabernacle and thinking they're on a little higher level than the rest of the race.

Directing priests' retreats for seventeen years has allowed me to see how wounded we priests are because of that inflation. We become inflated by reason of our private and public image. When that goes on for a long time, the remedy is going to have to be dramatic, because the illusion is so dangerous. This, however, applies not just to the clergy. A layman can have the same inflation on account of his job, his money, identification with his race, whatever makes him think he is better than the rest.

The procession back and forth from the Grail chamber

The strength and stability of the human person depend on maintaining a living connection between the center and the private self. Not an identification with the center, which is hubris; not an alienation, which tells us we are nothing, we are worthless, stupid. A living connection, rather, is the procession moving back and forth. And the procession does not stop. There will be alienation, but out of alienation comes yearning for union, and the process continues. Once we have had a Grail experience, our whole life is afterglow. But we forget that glow amid the hurly-burly of life and then we move back into alienation.

We in the West live in massive alienation from the center. So we try to create pseudo-Grail chambers by reason of role or title or money or prestige or religion — all the ways the ego can pretend to be at the center.

Every psychic and spiritual advance arises from the suffering of going on this journey, of then slipping back into the fall, back into defeat, separateness, non-union with the center, back into sin. The word "sin" is not a bad word. It is just that it has been so churchified that we've lost track of the gutsy meaning underneath. We better not lose the concept of sin, for without the pain of alienation or separateness there arises no yearning or longing. There is no space hewed out inside us for the Grail experience.

Then we rally and go back and taste the center for a while. God gives us little tastes. But there always remains the longing for the big taste. Transformation and conversion happen whenever energy is moved from the center to the private self, from the Totality (the consciousness and unconsciousness together, which is God) to our little conscious selves. These are the three figures forever coming out of the chamber with sword, lance, and Grail.

That's why the sacrament is always brought from the altar. At the heart of the sacramental experience is this movement to the center, the altar. At the altar is the energy or nourishment. Then there is the Grail moving from the altar/center to *us*. The symbols keep repeating until finally we believe we are that living connection: God comes to us from the center, and therefore it is okay to be little, a part, and at the edge. Or, as Merton better puts it, "The Center is everywhere and the circumference is nowhere."

At the center, that's blood

Few symbols are more potent than blood. It's ubiquitous in religion, very archetypal. Blood and its red color are at the heart of masculine spirituality. Without blood, spiritual movement does not happen. There are minor sufferings that fall short of drawing blood: We did not get our way; we suffered minor losses; our ego was bruised. Here, indeed, is where most men live their lives, with the trivial sufferings. But that's not blood yet, just a little weight on the soul, a little ego disappointment.

When religion gets serious, however, it draws blood. Religion is fascinated by the sword. What was Mary told? "A sword is going to pierce your heart" (Luke 2:35). Until the sword pierces the heart, until blood is shed, the profound thoughts are not revealed, the truth is not real.

Blood, in this context, is the intense and consciously allowed pain of realigning oneself with what is real. The price of getting back into the Grail chamber is to get realigned. To live with what is, not what we want things to be.

A dear one is dead. We don't want it to be; it isn't just; but it is reality. There's no fairness in the world; she did not get time to live a full life; but this is reality. It is an encounter with the left hand of God. It feels like injustice, like absurdity, it's Jesus sweating blood in the garden — always blood. We never get realigned with the Grail chamber, with the real, without spilling blood. It says that in Leviticus: There is no salvation except by blood (17:11).

In all religions it has historically been the private self, the little guy, who had to spill his blood to get realigned. There has always been blood sacrifice for this purpose. The Aztecs, for example, killed their own people for human sacrifice. The Jews killed animals, ten thousand heifers, twenty thousand goats, thirty thousand bullocks, great round numbers of them. That way God was supposedly pleased. Most other religions likewise forced the private self to spill blood to get back to the center. Self-denial, mortification, asceticism in various healthy and unhealthy forms.

In Christianity, however, in the person of Jesus, for the first time, the process was turned completely around. Here we had the center, God in Jesus spilling his blood so *he* can get realigned with *us*. This is a turning around of all religion! It dares to say, God is yearning for us. God is spilling the blood, God is opening the heart, so he can get out of the Grail chamber, so he can reach out to little Parsifal. Here is the key to the truth, and to the humanity, and to the transformative power of Christianity. To live with this, we had to create images like the Sacred Heart of Jesus. We have religious orders named after the "Precious Blood" and the passion, in recognition of this great mystery.

Herein lies the transforming union of the beloved and the lover. There is a price on both sides, but it is paid first by God. And because God knows we won't understand it conceptually, he does it visually and historically. Jesus becomes incarnate. God becomes a human being and walks the journey and ends up alone, bleeding at night, sweating blood in the Garden of Gethsemani, and the next day he dies on the cross. This exercises an immense transformative power on the soul — perhaps largely unconsciously.

The image we have given to this Jesus is the Lamb of God, in the Book of Revelation, chapters 4–6, the lamb slain yet victorious. There is related imagery in the Book of Exodus (12:1–14) — the first reading, as it happens, on Holy Thursday. The Israelites were told to go out to the fields and pick a perfect lamb. They were to bring it into their house on the tenth day of Nisan. It is easy to miss the point that they were to hold it in the house four days; then, on the fourteenth day of Nisan, they were to kill it. It's also easy to forget that if you have a lamb in the house four days, not only your kids but you yourself are likely to have fallen in love with it. It's a family pet after four days. What has to be killed (the symbolism screams at us) is pure and innocent and the last thing you would want to give up.

The lamb of God, therefore, represents the part of your life you will find every justification for holding on to and not spilling blood over. Your wife can't be the one to die. Your children can't be handicapped. Your job can't be the one to go. The trauma that comes to force us to align ourselves with the great mystery, with the great reality, will always feel, to a greater or lesser degree, like a lamb that's slain. That which is asked to die will always seem *good,* that part of ourselves that we have to give up usually looks innocent and necessary for our well-being.

Our Christian mystery says, in enthroning the slain and victorious lamb at the altar, that it is the only way through, that there is no salvation without the shedding of blood, without the great pain.

Two minor marriages

There are two minor marriages and a major marriage in the relationship we are trying to delineate.

One minor marriage is to the shadow. This is what Jesus is

talking about when he says we must love our enemies. The reason Western Christianity has not understood the love of enemies is because we have never understood the love of the shadow. First we need to learn it inside. We must learn to love our internal enemy. If we can't embrace and forgive our internal enemy, we will not be able to forgive the Russians or the Iranians or whatever group is today's evil empire that we are not supposed to love.

The other minor marriage is to the soul or anima or feminine — they're all synonymous here. The anima or soul is the doorway that opens us up to the inner chamber.

If those marriages happen, we'll be ready for the great marriage — the union with what is, the union with totality, with God. Thomas Merton gave a beautiful description of the great dance:

> For the world and time are the dance of the Lord in emptiness. The more we persist in misunderstanding the phenomena of life, the more we analyze them out into strange finalities and complex purposes of our own, the more we involve ourselves in sadness, absurdity, and despair. But it does not matter much, because no despair of ours can alter the reality of things, or stain the joy of the cosmic dance which is always there. Indeed we are in the midst of it, and it is in the midst of us, for it beats in our very blood, whether we want it to or not (*New Seeds of Contemplation*).

The dance is necessary because we cannot stay inside the Grail chamber. But neither can we stay outside in a state of alienation. All we can do is stay in the dance back and forth between inside and outside.

Gerald May says the same thing in his book *Addiction and Grace*. We cannot stay in a state of experiencing grace every moment. That's a pseudo-tower. It will only inflate us, and then make us rigid. The best we can do it seems is to persevere in the two-step: the dance between grace and addiction, where God always leads and we sometimes follow. We are, in fact, all fighting little addictions. Maybe it's some little mental pattern. Some small vanity. Or some little way of having our way. We try to be in charge, to grab a moment of control in a chaotic world. Those addictions can eat us up, those process addictions — even more than the drinkable addictions. The only way to give them up is through pain. We will not abdicate being central and important and right until pain forces us to do so. Until there is blood.

When blood is shed, things becomes clearer. Until Oscar Romero was killed, we did not understand what we Americans had done in El Salvador. Until there is a shedding of blood, we don't look. There has to be the martyr. Someone has to give his whole life to reveal the lie and expose the truth. Significant movements don't start until there is a hero to the point of shedding blood. Blood is the breakthrough. When we see how high the cost is, we realize how significant the truth is.

After Parsifal refuses to kill the Black Knight, Vassal, they become friends. Parsifal gallops back and forth endlessly on adventures, or in attempts to see Blanche Fleur or his mother. Once, in his wanderings, he remembers that it is Good Friday. This reminds him that he forgot his mother's advice, specifically her admonition that he go to church every day. And he has forgotten it for years, forgotten to go back to the center.

So he decides to go back to church. When Parsifal's story and the Good Friday story are juxtaposed, the symbolism is thicker and riper than usual. It is the day of the *axis mundi*, of the Tree of Life, when the blood flows and we know what is real and what is significant. We break through the illusions of the system to what is meaningful in life.

Parsifal, because he has not obeyed his mother, has to go to confession. He looks for a priest to whom he can confess. He finds a hermit in the woods. And hermits, mythologically speaking, are usually magicians.

Or try a magician

Basically, the magician is the image in our souls of awareness, growth, and transformation. It is the most complex of all the archetypes, because it has eight or ten major faces and forms. The hermit is one of them; the prophet another. In Christian mythology, the hermit's was the face of the magician most often presented. Otherwise, indeed, the magician was a dubious character because of problems we traditionally had with black magic. But we trusted the hermit.

The hermit, first of all, usually lived in the woods. And that's where Parsifal finds his hermit. Another characteristic of the hermit is that, traditionally, he was not married; he was a celibate. We need to rediscover the historical and healthy meaning of celibacy. Celibacy did not emerge by accident. The concept and practice are degraded by the unhealthy reasons, social and political, for which the church once mandated it. But there is something more at work here than those historical circumstances, something archetypal. That is probably why, deep down, the church is holding on to it.

What we're dealing with in celibacy is the archetype of the hermit. He is the one who has the totality within himself, by himself. He is in touch with nature and God and comes out of the forest and tells the truth. He's the archetype of wholeness, with the masculine and feminine blended together so well that he does not need a wife. That's the archetype, whether the modern age honors it or not. It's constant in religion. It's not just for celibates. There must be a hermit part in all of us.

To be true to this hermit part of the self, those who are married need to know who they are apart from their wives, or they don't know who they are. We have to be able to walk our journey and establish our personal meaning and even find God without using the wife to tell us every night that we are wonderful. If we run too quickly to union with the woman, this can keep us from the great union, from our inner hermit.

Most men I have met who had an authentic Grail experience admit there is 5 to 10 percent of themselves they can never give to their wives. It is given to God. This does not imply withholding anything from one's wife. Rather, it enables us to be faithful to our wives and love them forever with depth and power and truth. We now have something to give her beyond our private little self. We do not have a lot to give if all we have is our private self.

If a man has loved God deeply, has been in the Grail chamber, no sexual relationship will *fully* satisfy him afterward. It is not that he can no longer love. The body will continue calling out, wanting what the body wants, union. But now he knows and must say to himself, "Wait, wait, this isn't it, yet, there is something more." He can't become a sexual addict because he is balanced by soul and spirit.

I was once talking to a group of Protestant ministers, and a minister raised his hand and said: I've been envious of Catholic priests all my life. First, because you have so much more freedom, without wife or children. But what really annoys me is when you walk into a group of people, even Protestants, they are inevitably more in awe of you than they are of us.

I agreed with him that I had experienced the same thing. Why is it? I asked him. We can be as messed up as clergy in any denomination. And then he said, "It's the archetype of the hermit."

There is the impression that, because one lives alone, one has touched the mystery. It might not be true, but that's what the archetype hints at. A celibate is in the position to "wear the mantle" from which power comes (often in spite of ourselves!). Archetypes don't have to do with truth; they have to do with power, a power that comes out of one in the form of grace and life for others.

Bottom line, we want a king

When I teach at the jail, there is one session the inmates like best of all. I ask those guys, mostly Black and Hispanic, who is a king, and they almost without exception say John Kennedy. Why John Kennedy? Of course, we Catholics, especially if we're Irish, have easy reasons to be proud of our Irish Catholic president. We have since learned that he had a succession of women on the side and was less than perfect, but to the dudes in jail and many others, that does not matter. He was a king. We didn't call the early 1960s America Camelot without reason. Kennedy put out an energy that held a whole range of reality together. There had not been another president like that since Lincoln.

None of this stands up to rational scrutiny. We later found out his personal flaws, but at that moment John Kennedy carried king energy for this country. People had great visions. It was not a sick kingdom in the early 1960s. Young people were going off to the Peace Corps. There were multiple manifestations of idealism, not just in words but in practice. So different from the selfish 1980s. That's what a king inspires young men to do. He inspires big visions, because he is holding the world together so gracefully and so powerfully that the young man feels his energy and power.

The same is true of the magician. I am aware of my personal sinfulness, yet I cannot deny that I wear the mantle of the magician. I am being used somehow for the transformation of people. It would be a sin for me to deny that; it would be some kind of false humility. If you have the gift, you have to use it. Each man has his mantle, which he has to learn to wear with grace and dignity. That's masculine energy — to carry out what he has been given to do. To do otherwise would be unfaithfulness to the Lord of the Grail castle. To think it is *you* would also be unfaithful.

So, Parsifal meets the hermit. It turns out that the hermit is his uncle. He is, as it were, related to this magician energy. He already has a connection. What the hermit gives him is, finally, the right question, and then he sends him back to the Grail castle.

The question, he tells Parsifal, is: *Whom does the Grail serve?* And he tells him further: You go that way, and don't stop. That's what the hermit, the magician, finally does — tells us the direction of the path. First, he had to learn the direction of the fall, from the godfather, Gournamond — how to fall gracefully. In the second stage he had to learn the path of the return. Here, the language is faith, perseverance, trust. You don't know, you're just obedient. The hermit just calls you to obedience. Like responding to Obi Wan Kenobi in *Star Wars*, who just says, "Do it."

The young man wants answers, clarity, explanations. The man who, like Parsifal, has walked forty years in a circle is sick and tired of being sick and tired. He's ready to settle for less than total clarity. He's ready to believe the prophet when he says, "Here's the question and here's the path to follow."

Such a pilgrim will probably take some wrong turns, but that's why we speak of a spiritual "director." Nowadays, directors are modest and even apologetic about being directors — "I'm just walking with you," and so on. This is probably fine in the early stages. But when it's time to put in the lance, to do what hurts, we are going to defend ourselves and strive to get back to our comfort zone. We will go into denial, refusal to realign our lives with the clear, hard truth. I will not accept the bleeding lance in my heart. I will not let go of the drink or the toys I have accumulated or the self-image or any of the things I rely on to make me real. I don't want the real; I want my ego.

Ernest Becker calls that "character armor." It is character armor that finally keeps us from God; I don't think it is the shadow at all. In Christianity especially, we have acted as if it's the shadow that keeps us from God, but it is rather our attachment to our self-image, our unwillingness to move beyond denial, our defending ourselves against reality.

The best ally of God is reality. The heart suffers terribly

when it refuses to accept what is. Either we accept the necessary and limited suffering of realignment with the real, or we eventually incur years of greater suffering in lost relationships, job, self-esteem, and disunion with God. Spiritual common sense, which unfortunately is not so common.

So Parsifal returns to the Grail castle. He again witnesses the procession coming out from the Grail chamber, and when the man comes out with the bleeding lance, he takes it this time. Here is the blood coming out from the center — the Christ image. Notice the reversal. Before, we were shedding blood to get into the temple; now, God is shedding blood to get out of the temple. God comes to us.

The poison and the antidote are the same thing. The folks in the Book of Exodus already knew that. When the people in the desert were being bitten by snakes, Yahweh said to Moses, put a snake on a staff and hold it up (it is the physician's symbol to this day), and whoever looks on it will be healed (Numbers 21:8–9). False suffering is healed by true suffering. We tend to stay at the level of minor suffering and think it's conversion. But when the great lance comes, and the blood is spilled, these can move us into major letting go, major shaking off of our illusions. Nothing else in our culture is capable of doing this for us. None of us are capable of it without the Spirit, without a Grail experience. The wound is the gift, the gift is the wound — that's what the bleeding lance is saying, the lance of Christ that opens the outflow of blood and water.

In traditional pictures of the saints there used to be an arrow going into the heart. It signified pain, yet it was also liberation. There was a picture of St. Teresa of Avila with a little Cupid pointing an arrow into her heart. Until the heart opens up, there is no redemption. My faith is that we all get what we need to grow up, and we keep getting it until we get the point — sometimes that means many bleeding lances.

Suffering happens, healing follows

Parsifal now takes this bleeding lance — signifying the perpetually bleeding lance of God spilling his blood for us — and touches it to Amfortas, the wounded king.

Healing happens on about three levels at that moment. Amfortas is revealed in some stories to be Parsifal's father, so that relationship is healed. And Parsifal is, of course, now a son in touch with his primal nobility ("from God"). It would also be interesting to pursue the apparent theme of the son sometimes healing the father.

Secondly, his king energy is restored, and with it his kingdom. Until we stay on the journey to the spilling of blood, we don't understand. The kingdom will not be healed until it moves beyond the denial of its illusions and realigns itself with reality.

No sooner is the kingdom healed than plants start growing, the water flows, harmony returns, because we have realigned ourselves — at the price of blood — with what is good, what is true, with reality.

At that moment, after the king has sat himself on the throne, Parsifal says to him, "Whom does the Grail serve?" This king has been living in the castle, with the Grail, but seems not to have known the score. So Parsifal is asking not only for himself but for the sick king, who has been living for himself, the old man tied up in his own world.

And Parsifal says to him, in effect, what was your kingdom *for?* What is your kingship about? (Again, the son having the healing question for the old, tired men.)

The question is a timeless one. Presidents, we may ask, what is your kingship for? Popes, what is your kingship about? Fathers, what's your kingship about? What's your authority for? It's not for itself. It's for service. It's for the children of God, for the world, for the earth. It's for everything else. It's not so you can feel good about yourself.

Today, people have masculinity confused with patriarchy. What we are saying in the men's movement is that they are not the same. Patriarchy is the false king, who has not asked the Grail question. Patriarchy is the world of men who just want to get reelected and will tell any lies we are stupid enough to believe. And when we are stupid enough to believe those lies, we are dark kings, too. Dark kings, because we don't love the truth. We have not walked the Parsifal journey. We're satisfied with the king sick on his throne because we ourselves are sick out there in our private little world.

A man who once sees the truth will not accept dark kings and will not believe their illusions. We live and seem to thrive in a world of slogans like "It's good for the American economy," or "It's morning in America." And these are mouthed by people who think they are Christian. No one has told them about the path of the fall. Or about the path of the return. Because, you see, we're just Catholics, and not journeymen.

And that's why we are in a state of spiritual emergency. We cannot be satisfied with being just Catholics or just Methodists or just Quakers anymore. We need people who have been pierced through the heart like Parsifal. People who are prepared to go the distance and be perfect fools.

We need, in other words, the final clear recognition of what the center is, what the totality is, and how we are a part of it, and how our destiny is knowing, loving, and serving God at the center, and knowing that the center always comes toward us before we come toward it. That's the dynamics of grace — the procession from the Grail chamber.

The Grail king dies shortly thereafter, and his place, at least in some of the myths, is taken by Parsifal.

So the classic monomyth of the hero is: the departure, the journey, the encounter, and finally the return. It always comes back full circle. We go back where we began and, in the idiom of T. S. Eliot, know the place for the first time.

The Fisher King is what every man moves into: death and emptiness and woundedness by the time we're fifty, if we have not walked Parsifal's journey. He is a warning sign, a wake-up call, to men who are still young enough to change.

And now Parsifal sits on the throne because he has become the king, but he is not going to be the wounded Fisher King, simply fishing in the unconscious. Why?

Because he walked the walk. Walked through the terror, through the grief, went into the descent and accepted the lance. To use our recovery language, he finally moved beyond denial. When you're a good warrior and a good magician and a good lover, in submission to the king, you're a king too.

Parsifal lives in the Grail castle and marries Blanche Fleur and lives happily ever after! He is now remembered as the greatest knight ever to sit at the Round Table. In the circle. That is, one of the people. If you can't be one of the folk, if you've always got to be Dr. so-and-so, Fr. so-and-so, real people will not be impressed by you or trust you. True kings can descend from their thrones, free to be one of the human family. For now their throne is within and nothing without can threaten them.

The mystery of faith

St. Augustine said that our Christianity comes from our baptism, not our ordination. Ordination is simply a function for building up the body. It does not constitute anyone's identity. We are all equal in our baptism into the mystery of the dying and resurrection of Jesus. We call it the paschal mystery. This is the main event that we proclaim at the center of every Eucharist.

The mystery of faith is mythologically presented. Christ has died; therefore at least half of life will be absurd, unjust, painful, will make no sense to ego-consciousness. And Christ has risen; therefore half of life is beautiful, ecstatic, and sweet. This living and dying, good and bad, is all around us. It's the death and life we see everywhere in nature.

Christ has died, Christ has risen — the inexorable wheel. Don't try to stop it, get on it. It's the dance. You ride it.

You trust it. You trust the dying. You trust the rising. You live the dying. You live the rising. And Christ will come again and again and again. We cannot and we must not get off the wheel. Christianity is not about being "good"; it's about solidarity with Christ in both journeys: death and resurrection — again and again.

Jesus said the rich man cannot enter the kingdom of heaven because riches are a symbol of the attitude that thinks you can get off the wheel. Because you have a nice home in Arizona. Or friends in high places. What the rich man tries to do is climb to the up side of the wheel whenever it turns down. This doesn't work. He must take his turn all the way around the wheel. Pain and ecstasy are the teachers of the soul. Jesus leads us on the path.

Holy fool is a neat guy

In this final stage, the dominant image is the holy fool. He can let the wheel go round, can deal with it at the top or the bottom. He can laugh at both sides. The old man who cannot laugh is a damn fool, the wrong kind of fool. The holy fool laughs out of freedom. If we are still rigid, still checking everything out for orthodoxy, we're certainly no kings, and no holy fools. This is not new language: St. Paul used it a lot (Romans 1:22; 1 Corinthians 4:10; 2 Corinthians 11:19). He called himself a fool for Christ. Today, we might call it going for broke.

At the very time, a couple of years ago, that I started preparing this material, I learned I had cancer. I was told I had two to six months to live. Today, I'm fine. But now, I have my sacred wound — a big cut in my leg and groin. I'm so grateful for it. I envisage God saying, if you're going to talk about this stuff all the time, I'm going to emblazon it on your body. Your physical wound will remind you that you are wounded at the core.

Once you have faced that big demon called death, that

helps you go for broke. (It was only for a few weeks that I thought I was going to die before I was told I would recover again, so I don't know if I completely faced death deep down inside.) That's what baptism is supposed to be: facing our dying ahead of time, early in the journey. This early rendez-vous with death supposedly helps us to know what the real issues are, what is worth spilling blood for, what truly lasts. Anyone who has faced death can attest that he was different afterward. We feel more like going for broke. We feel more like playing the holy fool. A lot of things we worried about before just do not matter anymore.

During those few weeks I thought I was going to die, all that mattered was what and whom I had loved. Not what I had thought. Or my own virtue, or my well-worn formulas or dogmas. Rather, the issue is: Did love happen? Did communion happen? Did any kind of surrender to truth take place on the journey? That's the only thing likely to give you comfort and joy at the end.

That's what the fool knows. Normally you do not become a fool without (1) facing death and without (2) falling in love. Unless you have fallen in love, you probably won't be able to face death without great anguish. You would have no way of trusting the great passover. No assurance there is Anyone over there to receive you — Anyone called Love.

Love grounds the whole thing. It is the foundation of all reality. When we have loved enough, we can face death without fear. I think that is the heart of all religion. It certainly is the heart of Christianity.

Chapter 8

Promises to make and keep _____

(The retreat is drawing to a close. A group of over a hundred men is gathered in a great circle. They have spent several days sharing their lives and inner thoughts and souls, and this is their last night. The aim now is to find closure, conclusions; to make new promises, resolutions. It is a time of participation, loose, the key is openness. Of the men who speak up, space and circumstances allow for only a very small sampling here.)

I have no lecture planned for this time. We need, instead, to discern. Let what needs to be said get said.

There are three gates, three tests, through which our words should pass. First, is what is said true? If it's not true, of course, we should not want to say it. Second, is it loving? This is not the same as being nice or polite. Rather, is it going to build up life? Third — maybe the most difficult of all — is it necessary?

One thing that characterizes the wise man — I notice it when I visit among the Native Americans — is that he is usually rather quiet. Many of us may have noticed this with regard to our own fathers. They wait and listen, and when they speak they have something to say. We should, at this time, aspire to that kind of discernment — not to squelch expression but to refine it so that what gets said is the best.

Man:

For the so-called civilized man the spiritual world lies below the surface, and the problem is to dig down and find it and then let it out. Yesterday, I went to the mountaintop but I wasn't able to get quiet and let go, for whatever reasons, perhaps out of fear, perhaps because I was embarrassed to reveal myself to other people. Then, after listening to others sharing their experiences, I realized I had missed out on something important.

So, after lunch, I wandered up the hiking trail and I found a secluded spot. I then took off all my clothes. But as soon as I got completely naked, I realized I was right in the line of vision for anyone coming down the hiking trail! It bothered me a little, so I climbed another twenty feet up the mountain and planted my bare ass on a rock and breathed the incense of the mountain.

I sat there twenty to thirty minutes. I just came alive. I think I felt St. Francis there, about whom I know little, but I found myself trying to remember the St. Francis prayer, and I placed myself in God's hands. The only fearful moment I had sitting there on the rocks meditating was when I thought of rattlesnakes. I looked around, didn't see anything, and just placed myself in God's hands. It was a wonderful experience, a culmination of this week.

Rohr:

It is often said that Francis is the patron saint of exhibitionists because he stripped down on one famous occasion when he rejected his father. And at the end of his life he stripped again and asked to be laid naked on the naked earth. Francis was an Earthman, literally in touch with the world.

I'm always intrigued to find that on male retreats there is this fascination with getting naked. It happens every time. I don't encourage it; I don't discourage it, either. It's clearly a symbol of what your psyche is trying to do: get back to the naked core, honesty, simplicity, shedding of persona and baggage, vulnerability (rattlesnakes!), and total openness. Nakedness is not surprising, considering what we have talked about this week.

But we need to know what this nakedness is leading us toward. One route to this deeper knowledge is an openness to the world of images. There are a thousand ways to do this. Some find reading biographies useful, or watching good movies. Such an exercise should make us aware of various special people who for one reason or another fascinate us who thus give us juice or energy, make us feel alive — who compel us, in the words of Ecclesiasticus, to beat a path to their door.

Another route to self-knowledge is through the world of dreams. Dreams are our archetypes naming themselves and showing themselves to us. They are soul images that become passageways to spirit.

Times of prayer or meditation constitute a cleaning of the lens so the images can show themselves. If we lead an unfocused life full of diversions, we will not be able to grab on to these images, nor will they grab onto us. Our demons and our gods — using these words in their rich, broad sense — are our big teachers. There are archetypes that grab us negatively and others that grab us positively. We must listen to and learn from both.

We should utilize anything that will get us into a right brain mode, such as music or art. Those who can draw should trust the instinct to draw. When I teach this at the jail, invariably, a few days later, the sisters bring me a whole sheaf of drawings. The guys at the jail all draw pictures of what I talked about. Journaling is another sure help to self-knowledge.

And we should seek silence. We should aim to understimulate ourselves. In our usual overstimulated world, there are so many images and distractions that none of them grab us. None of them get a chance to become gods

or demons for us and therefore do not open the passageways to spirit. Jesus made it clear that we need this silence,
that we need to slow the world down so that the images can
grab us. In this quieter, more hospitable climate the images
can give us access to the holy.

Man:

I'm a Seven on the enneagram, so I don't like pain. This
morning was very painful for me. As I shared with my brothers, however, there was great healing and great strength. I
thank the group for that.

Man:

Richard's comment that when one faces death one knows
what the real issues are reminded me of a story. It took place
in ancient Japan. There was a tea master, very accomplished
in his art — and in Japan the tea master's art is regarded as
highly spiritual — who was assigned to a lord.

The lord had been summoned to another city for a conven-
tion. He invited the tea master to accompany him. The tea
master was upset because the city was infested with samurai mercenaries who would be looking for an opportunity to
put another notch on their belts at his master's expense. The
tea master had an uneasy feeling that he, too, could become
involved. He begged the lord not to require his company,
but the lord insisted. Not only that, the master demanded
that he go in the garb of a samurai. The loyal tea master had
no option but to follow orders.

In the city, he spent a week doing the tea ceremony ritual;
then he had a day off. He went downtown to visit a garden
he had always wanted to see. While he was there, he saw a
samurai mercenary. Unfortunately, the mercenary saw him,

too. The tea master tried to avoid the man, but the samurai insisted on a confrontation.

The tea master explained that he was not a real samurai, but had been ordered by his lord to dress up. He said he did not want to have a fight. The samurai, however, wasn't buying this story. So the tea master, resigned to impending death, made a last request of the samurai: "Please let me go back to my master and tell him what has occurred."

The samurai agreed. The tea master was walking back to the palace when he chanced to see a school of swordsmanship. He entered the school and found there the swordmaster who taught the samurai warriors. He described his predicament, then said to the swordmaster: "I only ask that you teach me how to die."

"In my entire career of teaching samurais how to kill," said the swordmaster, "nobody ever asked me how to die. I will do that, but first, tell me what your art is." The tea master explained.

In that case, the sword expert said, please fix me a cup of tea. The tea master embarked on the ritual of making the tea. The swordmaster stopped him in the middle of his intricate ceremony: "That's fine. Thank you." Then he instructed him on what to do when he went back to face the mercenary. "When you do all these things when you are with the mercenary, believe in your mind that you are doing your tea ceremony."

The tea master thanked him and went back to confront the mercenary. He did everything the swordmaster had told him. He knelt down, gathered his ceremonial robe beneath his knees as instructed, and raised his sword as he was instructed to do, all the while believing he was performing his tea ceremony. Before long, however, the mercenary fell to his knees, apologized, and begged the tea master's forgiveness. He begged the humble tea master not to kill him, for it was obvious that he was a superior samurai. Then the samurai ran away in terror.

What the story tells me is that if you can love who you

are, you can face death. And there is a tea master in all of us. If I pay attention to the tea master within me, I too can face any death. I am honored to be among men who are masters here today. And I thank Richard for being the swordmaster who showed me how to die.

Rohr:

We here are blessed people. We are, for the most part, just white, middle-class guys. It is pointless to go around feeling guilty for that. We have the time, we can fly here, take a week away from work. We're lucky. But this also creates a responsibility. We are the patriarchs of the world, the white males. That is both a gift and a new kind of burden, a truth we are trapped in.

What to do about the body?

It has been widely assumed, for some strange reason, that our souls are in our bodies. And when our bodies die — according to this scenario — our souls go to heaven or hell or somewhere else. But it seems much closer to the truth to turn things around and say our bodies are part of a larger world-soul.

Think of the body as an incarnation. Whether we consider the smallest level, the cell, or the largest level, the cosmos, this truth stands out. And why wouldn't it be true of all the stages in between. All these parts are swirling around one another. And each seems to think it is independent, but it's not.

Of all the world religions, Christianity has the biggest bias against the body. This is a disastrous theology. If I were Satan, and if I wanted to destroy Christianity, I would work overtime to tempt Christians to hate the flesh. Because we are the only religion that ever believed that God became flesh. Isn't that ironic?

The incarnation means that God moved from spirit to word to flesh. Jesus took on a body. He had genitals. He sweated. He defecated. It is an extraordinary leap to believe that God entered this world. And yet, as I have traveled the earth and seen different religions, I found we have the most negative attitude toward the body. Our bodies carry the most shame and guilt just for being a body. Maybe it's not so extraordinary. That's the way evil disguises itself. It turns the good around.

In our creed we say it boldly: We believe in the resurrection of the body. So, whatever God is doing, he is not doing it just in the spirit. He saves this thing, this composite — the only "I" you and I know. In this God is also liberating the body, even as we walk around and get older and decay, he is saving our bodies. And whatever happens eternally, this body is going to be a part of it. "I believe in the resurrection of the body."

We are reminded of this also at the Eucharist. When we put the bread in the mouth of the Christian, we do not say "Spirit of Christ" but "Body of Christ."

A mother once told me a story about her little three-year-old who watched the priest saying "Body of Christ" and eventually asked: "Does that mean Jesus's behind, too?" That's how real it gets. Almost cannibalistic, almost sexual. Taking the body inside. We're an incarnate religion. And terribly ashamed of it. And terribly afraid of it.

I think we're afraid because there's too much power involved, and too much truth. The body never lies. We speak of non-verbal ways of telling the truth. We can tell all kinds of lies with our mouth and even with our mind, even to ourselves, but the body tells the truth. The non-verbal reality gives it away. The body carries the truths of what I call our history of touch. Our bodies carry guilt, shame, inferiority. We meet very few people who are entirely satisfied with their body. There's always something we don't like about our physical selves.

Our bodies carry the pain of all the rejections we suffered, all the way back to when we did not make the team in the third grade. It carries all the betrayals, all the abuse — verbal, emotional, certainly sexual abuse.

We men are able to be out of touch with this, it seems, much easier than women. The woman is forced into acceptance of the body by menstruation and childbirth. Somehow women understand somatic, corporeal theology. They can acknowledge that bodies speak the truth, because they see a whole body come out of their own. And the miracle of that apparently transforms a woman forever. The woman can see that this body is already spirit.

We men don't understand that. We're disconnected from it. The father can implant the seed and literally leave. He does not experience the organic growing and the miracle come out of the body. I think that puts us in a handicapped position. We lag behind in understanding the body.

Another complicating, debilitating factor is the linkage between touch and sex. We don't know how to touch without the touch meaning or leading to sex. When we start touching, there follows a natural progression culminating in orgasm.

Some years ago, when counseling married couples, I used to encourage them to try, for three months, to find pleasure in one another while refraining from the urge to orgasm. They were invited to find delight in simply running the hand along the arm, for example, or to delight in the crevices of the hand, and behind all this to realize that simple touch gives delight to the other.

I know a man who spends his mornings at the hospital cuddling little babies because he believes in this power of touch. But that is not regarded as normal for men. I'm not sure how we got into this trap. One theory is that men are set back because they have to make the separation from the mother. It's a step in our initiation that apparently a girl does not have to go through.

And it is terribly difficult, the experts say, because we are entirely bonded with the mother. We have to break with her and transfer that identification to our Father. Maybe that's the beginning of the art of separation or the curse of separation. In any case we're afraid to touch, to move into any kind of concrete communion.

Jesus seemed to be aware of this and eager to do something about it. Much of his ministry involved touching people. It was never an antiseptic proclaiming of the word. He always combined the word with, for example, the laying on of hands. He sought physical communion with the person. He encouraged the woman washing his feet. A week later, he performed a similar action for his twelve brothers. At the same last meal he seemed completely comfortable with John's head resting on his chest.

One of the clearest indications of how homophobic and unnatural our culture has become is the fact that most of us could not imagine, in a group of men, one man leaning his head on another man's chest. Touch means sex for us, that's all. We don't know how to hold hands, we don't know how to connect, we don't know how to enjoy all those levels of human communion. We can't enjoy human intimacy with touch without it leading to orgasm. It's just scary to us. And that no doubt goes back to our long history of touch.

I once counseled a man who had a troubled sexual relationship with his wife. His story was not so surprising. One day, his mother had walked into the room, and there he was, playing with himself. Although he was only four or five years old, she screamed in rage, slapped his hands, and told him if she ever caught him touching that again she'd cut it off.

Now maybe this is an extreme case, but we can understand there was no way that man could trust his own penis after that, because the word from the goddess was that it was a dirty instrument, something to be loathed. As a grown man, all he could hear was shame, shame, and guilt about having a penis. In a true Christian culture we would not have to worry about such garbage.

I once spent several days in the Philippines with a young

Filipino Franciscan who at one point said, "I sometimes wonder why I became a Franciscan."

We were so free before you Christians came, was his gist. "Let me give you an example," he went on. "I hope this doesn't shock you, but when a young Filipino boy can first get the seed there's no shame associated with that. That first masturbation is a moment of glory and breakthrough. I know you won't understand this," the Filipino Franciscan said, "but I came running into the school yard with the seed in my hand. All my classmates came crowding around me and I exclaimed, 'I got the seed, I got the seed.' All the little guys were looking at it and this meant that I was a man. Now why would that be bad or displeasing to God?

"Then this old Franciscan walked up and said, 'What's that in your hand?' So I told him, 'It's my first seed,' and he said, 'Go wash your hand and don't come back.' And I could not understand. Why would that be displeasing? Why would the seed God put in our body be something I should be ashamed of?"

Most Filipinos, of course, like 95 percent of the people who have lived since the beginning of time, have lived in one-room houses, slept in family beds. They saw their parents make love. They saw their father's erection. They saw their mother's breasts. They observed one another as children — in many warm countries you don't put clothes on until seven or eight.

We of the West, on the other hand, grew up in antiseptic rooms. Our little babies are put in nurseries. We decorate the nurseries, but we shut the door, and the little boys grow up in these stark chambers. No wonder we're so curious. No wonder we live in such shame about our own bodies. When something happens to it we're convinced we're the only man it ever happened to. We live in an artificial environment, a kind of incubator. Not the way most people have lived — in a kind of natural connectedness with one another's bodies. We grow up with a general kind of shame about our bodies, certainly about our genitals.

When I gave retreats in Kenya, they took me to visit some of the Masai villages. Most of these Masai guys are seven feet tall. They'd come up to us with just a goat skin over the shoulders, that's all they'd have on. So imagine a guy seven feet tall, and keep in mind that I'm fairly short, and you can imagine what I find myself looking at! They had no shame about this — it never entered their mind. I was the one standing there embarrassed, trying to look somewhere else! We, clearly, are the ones with the problem. We're the ones who are unnatural and unfree.

Where did our fears come from? Those who are Five on the enneagram (i.e., very afraid of being embarrassed or exposed and consequently extremely circumspect as a defense mechanism) become Fives most likely because touch wasn't there when they wanted it. So we Fives decided to stop wanting it. Many Fives jump if you touch them. Touch is still something to be afraid of. Maybe there's a little Five in all of us. We just can't naturally surrender ourselves to experience reality through our bodies.

The Catholic Church used to define sacrament as an outward sign that gives grace. Tonight we are going to celebrate a sacrament. I regard it as the eighth sacrament, the one that got left out — the washing of the feet, the touching of the body and the communicating of the mystery through touch.

What people generally want to do, when confronted with feeling, is take refuge in their minds. Your mind is the control tower. Don't give in to the mind and try to explain it. And don't try to run away. Just try to experience it. Are you comfortable being touched? Don't answer me, but answer yourself. You probably answer: Yeah, but by a woman. But that's not the whole picture. Can you be comfortable simply with human touch? With the touch of another man?

Where does the fear come from? Where does the shame come from? It might help to look back at our personal history of touch.

Did we hear the words, "Don't touch yourself there" when

we were kids? Were we told always to keep our diapers or panties or clothes on? Was the family aghast when we ran into the living room naked, as little ones often do? What were the bathing practices? Did the door have to be shut? Were your parents ashamed of their own nakedness? I remember walking in on my mother nursing my younger brother and she was just horrified. She screamed and told me to shut the door. I must have been in kindergarten.

Then, later, when we have an opportunity for some pornography or peeping Tom experiences, we are naturally going to take them. And take them, at least in part, precisely because they are forbidden. What makes all this so unbelievably attractive is the taboo: There must be something really sweet there that I'm not supposed to see. When it is forbidden, we will surely want it.

For many, the problem with touch can be traced back to sexual abuse — the experience of 10 percent of any average group. That hurt requires its own treatment. It will have to be healed with the help of somebody, with the help of prayer, with a therapist, because the hurt is so deep when the body is abused.

For many others the problem derives from what was not done. Some actions are taboo in almost every family. Nakedness was taboo for many of us — the old Anglo-Saxon bias against the body. Probably burping and farting were not allowed. If they happened, we probably had to apologize. Apologizing is not a bad thing, but something about it says it's not okay to be a body.

Words, of course, especially those that described bodily functions or parts, were danger zones. Families make up cutesy substitute words. They're fine, but there is nothing wrong with calling things by their names, such as penis or vagina. The comfort of the parents in their regular speech tells the kids what is okay. If we did not grow up relaxed like that, we have probably still got fears and discomforts ourselves. There is nothing evil about this; it's just our history.

Where and when and in what kind of atmosphere were those discussions about the differences between boys and girls, boys and men, girls and women? Questions about where babies came from? Such discussions happen whether the adults are comfortable or not — teasing about body shapes and body parts and sizes, for example — and where or with whom they happen can have a lifelong effect.

And not just words but gestures. Remember when the patterns of affection switched and changed? Dad stopped hugging or kissing you because you were a boy. He started shaking your hand and told you to shake the hand of your uncles from now on. No more of this hugging or hanging on to them. There was an oblique but definite message.

One father from the Midwest told me he had three small sons, and they always wanted to be all over him. One day, one of them got aroused, just from body touch. From that day forward, he told me, "I never let them get close to me. It was only after I heard you talk that I realized it was my own feelings I was afraid of. I was getting aroused and I was thinking, 'My God, am I a homosexual?'"

No, just a human being. And when the male body is alive and in love, that's what happens. But the man said, "From that day I never let them come close to me." One can only speculate what message the boys received from this change of demeanor.

We are the sum of all the good and bad habits of our youth, of both appropriate and inappropriate incidents, of whether we were ever abused, of our youthful experiences of masturbation, pornography, locker-room talk, our own shame or otherwise about our growing genitals or pubic hair.

Some may feel a little shame even as I'm talking about this. My God, you're saying, what does this have to do with religion? He's supposed to be a priest and here he is, talking about pubic hair!

I never thought I'd be talking about it, either, until I found out how many people are wounded. And how many people cannot trust themselves to love in life, because there is this unbelievable shame. I hope you are listening to your own reactions as I say this. If you are wanting me to stop and get through this, that's saying something about you, something about your history of touch and your comfort with your own body.

Eating habits, too, reveal a lot. Our country is obsessed with being skinny. Consequently, many of us have endless shame about eating. So we eat in a hidden way because we're ashamed of our weight. Others feel skinny and scrawny.

Similarly, our early sexual experiences may haunt our relation with the body — the first, clumsy, amorous attempts, the shame or inferiority or inadequacy. And usually guilt comes trailing. Perhaps a confession experience was associated with it. Perhaps we shared the experience with someone and got laughed at. All those experiences formed the body we experience now, shaped the attitudes toward the body.

We believe in the resurrection of the body. We believe God loves the human body. The soul is not in the body, but this body is part of a larger world soul. We are men who, by virtue of the incarnation of Christ who took on a body, must honor our bodies as temples of God. We receive the body of Christ into our body and we exist in this world as temples. So this body is to be honored and tonight we each celebrate our own bodies and one another's.

During the first thousand years of the church's existence, the true body of Christ (*corpus verum*) was considered to be the membership, the people. The mystical body (*corpus mysticum*) was the Eucharist. The bread kept reminding the real body that it was the Real Body. In the second thousand years, our understanding was turned almost entirely around. We became the mystical body of Christ and the Eucharist became the *corpus verum,* the real body of Christ. I think the first thousand years is closer to the mystery of the incarnation. Amazingly, after all the centuries, we are still dealing with the shame of our own incarnation.

We want to heal that shame tonight as we celebrate the

great sacrament of the living body of Christ which we are, especially when we are gathered in this kind of faith.

(At this point, the hundred men who have been sitting in a circle around the edge of the huge room begin to take turns receiving a massage from the other men in the audience. When their age group is called out, the men of that group go to the middle of the room and lie down to await being touched and massaged by the other men. Every man has been given red tape and has placed this tape where he feels he stores wounds of some kind in his body. Some have their heads taped, others their hands or arms or chests or thighs. The men doing the massaging have been instructed to place their hands especially on the wounds of their brothers, to pray over them, bless them, and stay with the movement of energy. The men receive the massage, beginning with the oldest. Anyone who does not wish to participate is not required to, although all apparently do.)

Brothers, these are your fathers. Do not leave any father unattended. Surround them with your love. Let them feel. Let two or three of the younger men massage the elders. Touch them. Don't be afraid. This is the living body of Christ.

This is a man just like you. Who has his own fears. Imagine the burdens he has carried in fifty or sixty or seventy years. Imagine the moments of doubt. No different than your own. This man is your father, he is your grandfather, he is who you will be. The body isn't as young and fit now, but he was once a young man. Touch him and do not be afraid.

Pray over those wounds he carries in his body. Let him feel that you care. Men care, too. Not only women touch lovingly; men do too. You are his brother, his nurse, his friend, his companion, his lover, his brother. If you knew how good it feels from his side. He can feel your care. Look at the body of Christ loving itself. Look at the wounded soldiers, the wounded men, the men who have carried the wounds for years. The loves that didn't work. The body that is sometimes sick and weak.

May he feel your prayer, your caring. May he know he is

not alone. You can say it with your touch much better than I with my words. As you quietly finish, return slowly to your places. And you who have received the care, lie quietly and absorb the love you have received.

Believe what you have just received. Don't move into your head and begin to doubt or to rationalize. Just lie there and bask in the touch of a man; the touch of a brother; the touch of your sons, who perhaps often wanted to but never felt the freedom to touch you. You may rise now and return to your places. You are our elders, our fathers. You have been anointed.

Now, you who are aged fifty to fifty-five, take your places in the middle of the floor. Let us love you. Surround them, brothers, don't leave anyone unattended.

These are the would-be kings in their fifties. They want to put the strands of their lives together. They probably still carry the guilt of failures, the shame of mistakes. They have had their nights of self-hatred. Of anxiety. They had losses and betrayals and grief. Hold their grief. Touch them and believe that God's power comes through your touch. This is the body of Christ loving itself. This is the body reconnected. Don't be afraid. Nothing but good can happen. Energy, life, grace pass through your fingers. Trust that you are the body of Christ, an instrument. You are doctors, nurses, but better even than that.

Don't be surprised to feel your own energy draining out of you. This is hard. And yet it is wonderful. As you have completed giving your blessing, quietly, slowly, in your own time, return to your places and join in the circle of prayer. Bless your brother as you leave. He is God's man. You are all God's men, giving and receiving.

And you who are lying down, don't get up too quickly. Lie there and believe and trust what's happening. Is it too good to be true? A man you hardly know has touched you and maybe kissed you. Could this be the kiss of God? Could this be your father's kiss? Bask and believe. And as you wish, slowly, without losing the gift, arise and return to your places. Thank you, brothers, for letting us love you.

Now, those who are forty-five to fifty, let us love you. You who wish to heal, surround them, and leave no brother unattended. It is uncomfortable to bend or kneel and have energy flow out of you. You'd like to keep it. Go on, give it away. Spiritual energy only increases by being used, which is different than the case of purely physical energy. Give it away and you'll find more flowing out of your fingertips.

These are the brothers in the middle of life. Still worried about their marriages and jobs, wondering if life is going to be a success. Worried about their kids. Worried just like you are. Little men, just like we're all little men. But with big doubts, big fears. Sometimes with a hatred of self and body. Love them, brothers. Don't move into your heads; stay in your hearts, in your bodies. You can heal them. Don't judge, don't analyze, don't even think. That way, your body will be a clear instrument.

Jesus received similar healing when a woman touched his feet, although he knew all the men in the room were judging and analyzing. He just accepted the touch. If you could see yourselves — the body of Christ. When will this happen in any other place? Only the body makes it safe enough to be the body and live the truth. This is the way we were meant to live, but generally we are not allowed.

Pray over your brothers. Don't be afraid to touch them. Don't be afraid to bless them. Inside, they are saying, "Go away," and they're also saying, "Don't stop." As Scripture says, how good it is, and how sweet, when brothers dwell together as one, in a new kind of army, the kind of army the world cannot train, the army of healing and compassion.

You who lie on the floor, bask and believe. You have been healed by the body of Christ. Do not doubt the gift. This was your father, your son, your brother who touched you.

Slowly rise and return to your places. Do not go into your heads, but stay in the joy of your touched bodies.

Now, brothers between forty and forty-five, enter the center of the room and let us love you. Brothers, surround them. You may feel you're wearing out; you're not; there is still more love in you, more healing in you. Bend over, kneel to love. You have to kneel to love. You have to be a bit uncomfortable to love another. Some of you know now how good it feels.

This is Everyman. All the men who are living in lonely shacks tonight. Feeling useless and stupid, alone, separate, disconnected. You're not just loving this man; you're loving every man in his loneliness and pain. You're loving the universal body of Christ. Remember, brothers, no love is lost in the world. If it is going out from you, it is going out there, creating healing in the universe. Let it flow through you. No love is lost. Let it come out of you.

Touch this specific one brother in front of you. He is the suffering poor. He is the man lying sick in a hospital bed. He is the man who has been in jail for ten years, unjustly. He is the man who has been rejected by the woman he loved, and afraid to ever love again. He is the man who hates himself because he is gay. He is the man who hates himself because his body isn't right. He's the handicapped man, who just for one hour would love a perfect body and will never have it. Touch the pain of the world, touch the body of Christ. Wear the body of Christ. You are the body of Christ. No love is lost in the world.

Do not be afraid. Do not believe your fears. There is nothing to be afraid of. Do not doubt what God is saying. He has no hands but our hands. Outward signs that give grace. Do not doubt grace, do not doubt the sacrament. Quietly, slowly arise and return to your places.

Now, let those brothers in the middle of life, from thirty-five to forty, come forward. Let us be fathers to you. Let us be friends to you. Surround them, brothers. There is still more love in you, still more life in you. You will not run out, I promise you, the jar will not run empty.

Remember how afraid you were when you were in your thirties? You were not sure whether you were a man yet. You felt like you were still only a boy. You were not sure if you had any wisdom yet. You were still learning how to love your wife. Your children were still young. You didn't know if you were a good father; you didn't know if your children would reject you. Men are filled with fears in their thirties.

Tonight, you are father to these men in their thirties. You are their brother. You are their friend. This is a striking image of the church. This is the body of Christ. This is an alternative society. This is a new creation. This is what we were created for and our bodies know it. Giving love and receiving it. This is an instance of the reign of God. These are spiritual warriors, wounded and healing. This is the son you want to touch but in his thirties he does not have time for touch. He is just trying to be successful and he can't believe that touch could matter. Do not doubt the gift, brothers.

You on the floor, slow down, trust it. Believe what you are feeling. Don't move into your head; this is the only way God can get at you.

And you who are tending them; see where they carry their wounds. Imagine how much they hurt. Touch them, bless them. And when you have given your gift, return slowly to your places.

Brothers on the floor, don't get up too quickly, as we do everything in our thirties too quickly. Looking back, we wonder if we were ever thirty at all. Feel the grace. This is the sacrament. How many men throughout the world, if this could happen to them just once, would be elated and forever grateful.

Let us sit for a moment and listen to our bodies.

(*The participants shared their stories and reflections for over an hour, often with tears and groans, about the healing effects of this "laying on of hands."*)

Next morning: beginning of the Eucharist

And so Parsifal found the question, "Whom does the Grail serve?" And the answer that the wounded king gives is, "The Grail serves the Grail King." In the place of the Grail we have placed the globe of the earth. This is to remind us that all of this is for the sake of the world, the whole, the beyond, which, finally, of course, is the Lord.

What we have done here is not for our sakes only but for the sake of the world. For the sake of the next generation. For the sake of the sons and grandsons. Listen for the prayer in your hearts, brothers. The prayer of desire and thanksgiving, of yearning and intercession, for healing of ourselves and the world.

A prayer

Father, you have created us out of nothing, and we who were nothing are now something. We live on this earth, in this little moment of time, little grains of sand and yet sons of God. We thank you for such a privilege. We thank you for these moments, these days, for these mountains, this sky, these clouds and these animals. And these men.

Send them away with your grace and blessing and anointing. With new manhood, a manhood that is at least half of God. We thank you for the half that we hold, the half that is our masculinity, the half that is our sonship, or brotherhood, and our hoped-for fatherhood of the world.

Gospel reading

This is sometimes called the high priestly prayer of Jesus, his prayer for the world and his disciples at the Last Supper: "I pray not only for these, but for all those who through their words and their lives will believe. May they all be one.

Father, may they be one in us, as you are in me and I in you. So that the world may finally believe that it was you who sent me. I have given them the glory that you gave to me. That they may be one as we are one, with me in them and you in me."

"May they be so completely one that the world will realize that it was you who sent me and that I have loved them as much as you have loved me. Father, I want those you have given me to be with me where I am so that they may always see the glory that you have given me because I know, Father, that you have loved me before the foundation of the world" (John 17:20ff.). This is good news from the Lord.

From the homily at the end of the retreat

Whom does the Grail serve? The Grail serves the Grail King. Our lives are to be given for the world. We are to be men for others. Once we hear the Gospel, however, once we have been into the Grail chamber, we are destined to live in two worlds: the world as it is, which we might call power, and the world as it should be, which we might call love.

We have to take both worlds absolutely seriously. Love without power, without entering into the world of power and struggle and bureaucracy and Mickey Mouse, is only sentimentality. This is cheap and innocuous religion.

The ideal world of love is always before us like the North Star to guide, but one never really arrives, or needs to arrive, at the North Star. One simply needs vision, direction, and hope that it is all going somewhere.

However, power without love becomes brutality. And that's what every culture instinctively moves toward. The culture is no more than the magnified private ego. And just as the private ego works toward self-protection and self-aggrandizement, an entire culture or nation-state generates that same dynamic intensified a thousand times. Preserve the corporate ego. Preserve the corporate lie. Preserve the corporate illusion.

Once we have learned the truth, we are trapped in it and we cannot believe the world of power is adequate or that it is a correct response to reality. And yet, the masculine journey is always about power, redeeming the name of power, the meaning of power, naming it correctly. Uniting it with love.

We have chosen Jesus as our primary hero, and no one addresses the issues of power or domination more directly. One could read the whole Gospel as Jesus undercutting false power and standing insistently and constantly on the side of the powerless. He always takes the side of the victim, the poor, the minority, the oppressed, the little ones.

And that was the knight's code in the Middle Ages. His first promise was always to defend the powerless — the widow and the orphan and the poor and the weak. If we use this power that we have just been given exclusively for ourselves, we are false kings, false warriors, false magicians, and we certainly are not lovers. This is God's world. We arrive at this point on a continuum of billions of years during which God has been speaking, inviting, naming. We, in our turn, have been invited on the hero's path.

The only hero's story we can write is our own. We are surrounded by heroic examples, but our call is not to be St. Francis; it is to be Saint Bill or Saint David or whatever our name is. That is the only place you can be heroic — in writing your own story with courage, with persistence, taking the path of the fall gracefully, and taking the path of the return courageously.

At my feet I have a Navajo rug. The design is called the Yei design. In it there is an image of God as the ground of our being. The four little men are standing on God. And yet, this God comes up around the side and is also their equal; although he surrounds them, they stand on him; and the very heavens are his feet sticking up into the heights.

Only God holds the spear. This signifies that only God has the power.

But the clincher in this wonderful design is that we are gathered in "a community of the non-violent." On closer inspection one can see that all the men are holding spears, but none of the spears have points. The points aim toward the middle of the shaft and neutralize themselves.

They have found their power in God and do not need to protect themselves.

So, to live in God, to stand on the ground of the great Father's being, our violence will be taken away. And our violence is taken away when our fear is taken away. Our fear always emerges because we have something to protect.

We enter the Grail chamber and know it is a radically trustworthy world, despite all the minor tragedies with which we may have to live. In this basic trust we can lay down our spear and our shield and stop being either protective or attacking. Now we can live the truly non-violent life.

We will be preoccupied with our own security if we think no one else is gong to secure us. It's all up to us. That's the burden of modern alienated people — the idea that we have to do it ourselves because no one else is *for us*. Then we are necessarily egocentric or narcissistic. It finally destroys the soul, because it is not a true statement about *what is*.

We live with a foot in two worlds, the world of love and the world of power. Both are God's world. If God is still willing to love the politicians, presidents, and patriarchs of this world and is not destroying them, they too must still be good. They must still present possibilities. They must still be God's sons. So we can't hate anybody.

Don't waste a moment on hate. Love alone lasts. And no love is lost. What the spiritual journey teaches us is that in the end there is only love. And the foundation of everything, just like the ground of being in this rug, is finally love. That's the Grail experience: We're standing on love.

Dante, at the end of his journey through the *Inferno*, the *Purgatorio*, and the *Paradiso*, a journey that stands for the divine tragedy and comedy that is all of our lives, sees "the love that moves the sun and the other stars." That's the love that has been guiding him. Thus, love gets us started on the journey. Love is not given to us to help us solve our problems. Love, rather, leads us into our problems. When we love, we are going to be led into the pain of the world. Just as his mother, Heart's Sorrow, led Parsifal into the journey. It's love that leads you to quest and not to hide behind your picket fence.

Because love does not take away our problems but rather leads us into them, we are afraid of love. What it leads us to, however, is a final universal grounding love that we can trust because we know it is not all up to us. We do not, therefore, have to take ourselves so seriously. That is why we can laugh like the holy fool. And we do not have to secure ourselves, because we are radically secured — we are beloved sons in a benevolent universe.

How to get back to reality

After a privileged experience such as a retreat, some men worry about reentry into what we call real life. In response I usually tell this wonderful Grimm brothers story of the Dark Brother. (The Germanic myths, by the way, are gaining more recognition and becoming more popular than the Greek myths, because the Greek myths tend to put all men and women up in the heavens. The Germanic myths, by contrast, are full of little gnomes and elves coming out of the earth. They get us in touch with Earthman, which is where we want to be. We have been putting men up in the sky too long.)

In this myth there is a man, probably in his twenties, who has just left the army. He has no job, no identity. He is wondering what he is going to do. He is walking along the road and the Dark Brother comes up.

"Can you give me a job?" the young man asks him.

The Dark Brother says he will give him a job for seven years; and he will pay him well at the end of those seven years. But first, the Dark Brother says, "You've gotta go down." Down into the grief of things. Down into the underworld. We may have a glimpse here of what Scripture meant when it said Jesus descended into hell. He descended into the darkness of the soul, the shadow, the tears at the heart of things.

The Dark Brother leads the man down into the underworld and shows him three boiling pots. He tells him he must chop wood for seven years to keep these pots boiling. He must save all the wood chips and store them behind the door. And he adds a further rule: "Don't look at what is in the pots." (Now we know there's trouble in store because whenever there is a rule it's likely to be broken.)

The young ex-soldier starts chopping. He is about a year and a half into the job, carefully putting the chips behind the door, when he weakens and thinks, "I'm going to look in that first pot."

Wouldn't you know, it's his drill sergeant. The drill sergeant was the first man who took control over his life, told him what to pledge allegiance to, what were the absolute rules and formulas.

He puts the lid back on the pot and stokes the fire more diligently than before. Now don't consider it killing the sergeant; consider it stewing over the problem. He is coping with his father figures. Stewing over them.

After another year and a half, he opens the second pot and it's his lieutenant. Another father figure. He stokes the pot more robustly.

Finally, he opens the third pot. It's the big man — the general (the president and pope all rolled into one)! The ultimate father figure. The man who demands our absolute allegiance. The youth really stokes that one. For seven years he keeps stewing over his father figures — those who have given him the rules and named the real for him.

By this time, of course, there is a huge pile of wood chips behind the door. The Dark Brother returns and congratulates him for having done well. Put all the wood chips in a sack and I'll take you up to the upper world, the Dark Brother says. The young man does this but on the way complains, "I thought you were going to pay me."

"Don't worry, you'll be paid when we get to the upper world," the Dark Brother replies.

As they walk from the underworld, the world of suffering and grief, the chips of wood in the sack turn to pure gold. Your inner work, your wood chips, are pure gold. But only gradually do they move from the deep unconscious to conscious delight and wisdom.

The young man stays in an inn that night. He is very excited about all the gold he has. The innkeeper asks him what is in the sack. He replies proudly that it is a whole sack of gold. He is, in other words, naive, tells too easily what he thinks he has. Sure enough, as he sleeps that night, the innkeeper steals his bag of gold.

The Dark Brother returns in the morning and asks where the gold is. It was stolen, the youth has to confess, and he tells about spilling the beans to the innkeeper. A bad mistake, the Dark Brother admonishes him. He will have to go underground for seven more years. Next time, he adds, don't give away the gold so quickly, until it is your gold.

Don't give away your gold too quickly. Don't explain all this to your wife or fellow workers or friends or anybody until it is *your own* gold. Until it is your own experience. Don't try to change anybody. Your energy, not your words, changes people. It is your energy, your freedom, your ability to let go, to surrender and smile when you feel like saying shit. That's when they see there is something new about you, that there is gold in your sack.

Beyond that, I don't have a lot of advice for reentry. Just don't give away your gold. Until it is your gold — and that might take some time. Least said is probably best. Remember the three gates: Don't talk unless it is true; don't talk unless it is loving; and, finally, don't talk unless it is necessary. And even if we pass through these three — "the best things can not be talked about"!

Afterword

I ache in the places that I used to play . . .
But I feel so close to everything that we lost,
We'll never have to lose it again.

—Leonard Cohen, "Tower of Song"

It is only a matter of weeks since I wrote the foreword to this book. But I am now in a different world. The death of my mother in the meantime opened up doors and rooms I had never entered before: Grail chambers of a different kind, with new processions from behind a newly parted veil.

We buried her on the feast of Epiphany, the twelfth day of Christmas. Time and space have not ceased to offer epiphanies since her passing. Reason and prose have failed me, but I find myself writing "necessary" poems (as opposed to refined poetry) several times a day:

Jan. 9:   Mom, the breakwater
          Between time and eternity,
          My shores now exposed to the waves.

Jan. 11: Her dying, crooked body taught me sacrament,
          Built a swinging bridge
          Between mud and mysticism
          On which I will henceforth walk
          And weep — and wonder.

Jan. 12: Swells of gratitude and grief
          Coming from an endless ocean
          Washing my life clean — down
          To a first coating of joy.

Jan. 20: I edit the galley sheets of the "Quest"
Not knowing what the quest is.
Like Parsifal, I long for the Mother.

Jan. 21: Eleanore, you have become a new
Kind of Absolute,
Vying with God!
Surprising, numinous partner,
Opening up the other world.

Jan. 23: Back in the air,
On the road.
But more under the earth
With her (with Christ?).

I am beginning to understand many things for the first time. I now know why Parsifal's longing for his mother and searching for his father provide both the energy for the quest and the goal of the quest. I know now why we must "honor our father and mother." These bonds build the bridges that walk us through this world, and into the next.

For those who have no parents, or no bonds of love, the quest is undoubtedly energized by the desire and yearning for that relationship. Sometimes, as in the case of St. Francis, it gives the quest even greater urgency and vitality.

If the bonds of love are there, our parents literally take us with them. They carry us through the quest by promise and prompting. They carry us across the boundary with them when they pass over. Afterward, some essential part of ourselves is already over there — and no longer here. It is not anymore a matter of mere theological belief. The mutual love built a bridge, and we have somehow passed over along with them.

So much makes sense now, precisely by walking through what made no sense. Is this not what the Hebrews meant by Passover? Is this why many sing alleluias at funerals and the Irish dance at wakes? Is this not why Mexicans and Filipinos eat and drink on their parents' graves on *Día de la Muerte?* Is this why many Oriental religions are basically ancestor worship? Is this not the personal and convincing meaning of the acclamation that Catholics recite but rarely understand: "Dying, you destroyed our death, rising you restored our life"?

The ancestors, and parents in particular, pave the path, build the bridge by going first. (Perhaps this is why it is so abhorrent for parents to bury their own children!) Now I know that immortality is not a doctrine or mere hopeful wish. We are being pulled across by the pulleys of love, by the people we have loved.

Unless someone we love has made the great passover, as Jesus did for his friends, it's all theory, theology and debate about immortality. When one has accompanied a beloved through passion and death, particularly the generation ahead of us (parents) or the generation behind us (children), resurrection is a living experience and reality. Love, the eternal thing, shows itself to be stronger than death.

At last I understand why Jesus said, "Unless I go, the Spirit cannot come" (John 16:7). The letting go of a beloved to God means the beloved takes part of you along, and sends some of the other world back. Each generation builds the bridge for the next to pass over. Finally, by my mother's death I have experienced "the communion of saints," which I always said I believed.

Wonderfully, it seems to work both ways. In the last months of mother's six-year bout with cancer, the love of family and friends also built a bridge for her. Streams of visitors, relatives, prayers, calls, meals, cards, long forgotten neighbors, offers to "do anything," hospice nurses and volunteers, ministers of communion from three different parishes all rushed to create "communion" and build the bridge for Mom's journey across. How lonely and frightful it must be if one is not part of a community of faith and love.

In her final days she said several times, "I am already in heaven." When we asked her if she knew that we loved her, she said without hesitation, "I know you do!" (She had not always believed that, being an impregnable Eight on the enneagram!) Mom even saw angels several times and had no need to prove or explain them to us. It was just taken for given. When I asked her if she was afraid to die, she said, "No, because your tapes taught me that I did not have to be afraid."

In a moment, too many tapes were all worthwhile. I knew it was her first unconditional love that set me out on the further quest for God. Now her receiving of my love brought my journey full circle, even before its time. All I had said in this book about the eternal feminine was true: Mary as Mother, Mary as Pietà, Mary as Mediatrix all became archetypal images, and no longer mere statues.

I asked her in her final comatose state if she knew who I was. She spoke quietly but distinctly, "You are Dickie boy, Eleanore's son." No one could know how that would hear, except my ears! The woman with the Grail had again proceeded from the Grail chamber, and God exploded from his hiding place:

> Dickie boy had never died
> He just hid under the covers
> Waiting to peek out and
> Again see Mother's face shine!

Like Parsifal, I can only undress, bathe, and go to sleep. She drew me across the drawbridge, and now it can snap closed behind me. The quest has a goal and the Grail is real. All we need to know, all we want to know, is that we are indeed "beloved sons."

The mystery of accompanying my mother through her passion, death, and resurrection made me know that I am truly a part of the Great Parade. (I remember being taught that the Gospels were initially mere passion and resurrection narratives — nothing more was deemed necessary!) I am finally in line and part of all the generations ahead of me. Hopefully I am lowering the drawbridge for those who are coming after me.

When you truly and fully *belong*, it is so natural to believe and to become. The tragedy of our time is that so very many do not *belong* (no parents, no family, no community, no tradition). No wonder that it is hard to *believe*, and survival takes the place of *becoming*. One true love is all that is necessary. It tells us we do belong, we are related, we are connected, we are at home. It's really okay. I am *in*, precisely because I have been led *through*. If the quest is not saying that, it has not said anything.

We grow by giving up. We learn by letting go. But someone's smile must assure us at beginning, middle, and end, or we will not surrender. That is the function of good myth and bonds of love. They create one another — and they re-create us. I hope this small book offers you both — good myth and enduring bonds of love.

Appendix

The enneagram as clue
to who we are

by Clarence Thomson _____

Occasionally throughout this book, Richard Rohr mentions people's enneagram numbers in order to describe or predict some of their characteristics. Most of the people attending the retreat on which the book is based were versed in the enneagram and knew their own numbers and probably the significance of other numbers as well. Not all readers may share this knowledge.

The enneagram is a popular personality typing system. In the enneagram theory of personality, each of us has a central compulsion or preoccupation created by our way of paying attention, of searching for or avoiding certain things in life. Each personality type has one chief characteristic and from this central trait a whole network of smaller preferences, outlooks, and tendencies can be inferred.

Briefly, each of the nine numbers can be described in a thumbnail sketch. This sketch is less than an introduction to the enneagram, but it will explain a bit why Father Rohr makes the allusions — often light-hearted ones — to particular numbers in a particular context.

Type One, which Rohr acknowledges he himself is, is the moral perfectionist and ethical reformer. Ones tend to have an unacknowledged anger, to be critical, especially of themselves, and to see life as a theater for moral heroism.

Type Two is the quintessential helper, who goes through

life meeting other people's needs while not acknowledging his or her own needs. Twos are the most interpersonal of all the types, being largely concerned about the quality of relationships at all times. If they are needy, they can't admit it, so they have a tendency to become manipulative. If healthy, they are sweet, almost seductive, and unbelievably forgiving.

Type Three is the success-oriented, high-energy, super-achiever that is the American hero. Threes put their emotional needs on hold and try to win love through performance. They are socially astute, being able to project the image of whatever it is the situation needs. If unhealthy, they are unfeeling workaholics. If healthy, they get in touch with love and other personal values.

Type Four is the tragic romantic artistic type. Fours like to be with other fours (in artists' colonies, for example) because they feel no one else can really understand the depth of their emotions. Their compulsion is to be different, special, to be authentic and take the emotional component of life more seriously than the rest of life. They have a curious ability to wallow in pain, feeling that pain has the power to make them emotionally deeper than others.

Type Five is the detached, observant, intellectual who approaches life as a spectacle to be watched. These are the people who get labelled "ivory tower" types because they prefer to keep their distance from the hurly-burly of life and reflect on it instead. The academic world is full of Five professors who specialize in footnotes. When healthy they are the finest of thinkers and researchers and have an unequalled intellectual depth.

Type Six is the fearful person who sees every situation in terms of what could go wrong. Sixes are ambivalent about authority, both fiercely loyal and suspicious of it. They love keeping the group together (family, team, order, any group) and so tend to want all the laws enforced so nobody in the group strays from the center.

Type Sevens are fun-loving, high-energy persons who often have a problem growing up because they avoid pain with too much ardor. If unhealthy, they are addicted to any kind of pleasure — food, sex, drugs, enjoyable work, art — and tend to be dilettantes. If healthy, they become renaissance persons because of their wide range of interests and vitality.

Type Eight is the person who considers the world to be about power. Eights are enormously powerful themselves; they scorn weakness and constantly put pressure on people to see if they will crack. Paradoxically, they are the champions of the underdogs in their world and devote huge amounts of time and talent seeing to it that the little ones get justice.

Type Nines are the peace-seekers of the world. They want no conflict and so they keep a low emotional profile, not committing themselves to any position until all turmoil related to it is over. They are the most passive aggressive, people-pleasing among the enneagram types. Their problem is a certain spiritual indolence. They may work hard to cover up the fact they are not taking care of the central spiritual concerns of their lives.

Even though it is necessary to describe probable behaviors, the real heart of the enneagram is one layer deeper. The nine types are really nine energies. Nine motives. Nine worldviews. Any number can do anything, but the reasons for doing it will be different.

Clarence Thomson is editor of the Enneagram Educator, *based in Kansas City.*